Agile Anchors:
The Scrum Master's
Guide to Business Impact

By

Lynn R. Squire

Table of Contents

Introduction: The Hidden Power of the Scrum Master

In most organizations today, the title "Scrum Master" is familiar, yet its true potential is often misunderstood. Many still see the Scrum Master as the person who schedules meetings, enforces ceremonies, or ensures that the Scrum board looks tidy. This limited view obscures the actual impact of the role.

A skilled Scrum Master is not simply a process facilitator but a business enabler who translates Agile principles into measurable outcomes. They help organizations transition from performing Agile to being Agile, where adaptability, focus, and value delivery become integral to the culture rather than a checklist.

As companies strive to stay competitive in an unpredictable world, the need for this kind of leadership has never been greater. Markets evolve quickly, customer expectations shift, and teams are more distributed than ever. In this environment, organizations succeed not just by moving fast but by learning and adapting continuously. The Scrum Master helps make that possible. They strengthen the connection between strategy and execution, guiding teams toward outcomes that align with organizational goals.

Over the past decade, Agile maturity has advanced across industries, yet leadership gaps remain. Many teams adopt Agile tools, but often fall short of consistently delivering value. Some Scrum Masters struggle to expand their influence beyond their immediate teams, while executives often fail to connect Agile performance with strategic goals. This book addresses that gap. It explores how the Scrum Master can grow into a strategic partner, one who not only drives effective delivery but also ensures that each iteration aligns with the organization's direction and objectives.

Agile Anchors: The Scrum Master's Guide to Business Impact offers a practical, experience-driven approach to understanding this transformation. Drawing from established Agile frameworks, real-world case studies, and insights from thought leaders, the book reframes the Scrum Master's role as a force that connects people, process, and performance.

You will discover how to translate Agile metrics into business insights, how to guide teams toward high trust and high output, and how to work with leaders to create genuine alignment between delivery and strategy.

Throughout these chapters, the book highlights the Scrum Master's evolving responsibilities in modern contexts: hybrid teams, AI-assisted environments, and large-scale implementations. It demonstrates how to maintain agility at scale, preserve the essence of Scrum under pressure, and use data ethically and intelligently. More importantly, it teaches how to build influence without authority and to lead from within the system rather than above it.

If you are a Scrum Master seeking to elevate your impact, an Agile Coach mentoring others toward strategic awareness, or a Project Manager looking to apply Agile principles more effectively, this book will help you bridge the gap between team-level activity and business-level outcomes. This book can be a perfect guide for anyone who wants to connect Agile practices to organizational success. Executives and leaders will also find value here in understanding how to partner with Scrum Masters to unlock agility across the enterprise.

The goal of this book is to deepen your understanding of how Scrum can serve not only as a delivery model but as a business strategy. By the end, you will see the Scrum Master's role as a catalyst for adaptability, innovation, and measurable business value. Their hidden power lies in their ability to align purpose, people, and progress, and this book is your guide to mastering that power.

Chapter 1: Agile as a Business Strategy, Not Just a Delivery Model

Agile was once viewed as a project management technique for software teams. Today, it has evolved into a strategic capability that helps organizations remain adaptable, innovative, and customer-focused in unpredictable markets. When implemented thoughtfully, Agile reshapes how companies plan, execute, and learn.

This chapter explores how Agile extends beyond delivery cycles to influence strategic thinking and decision-making. Drawing on current research and examples from industries such as finance and retail, it highlights how organizations are using Agile principles to align operations with business goals and build resilience in fast-changing environments.

Rethinking Agile Beyond Project Delivery

Agile's evolution over the past two decades reflects a shift in how companies approach change. The Agile Business Consortium describes agility as the ability of an organization to "sense and respond" through continuous alignment between strategy and execution. Their Agile Strategy Framework defines strategy as an iterative process—planned, tested, and refined in short cycles instead of fixed annual reviews. This model promotes adaptability in volatile conditions where traditional strategic planning often fails[1].

Agile was born in software development but quickly became a management philosophy used across industries.Recent academic research confirms the value of this approach to organizations.

A 2024 *ResearchGate* study found that companies adopting Agile at the enterprise level experienced higher customer satisfaction, improved risk visibility, and stronger innovation rates. Respondents highlighted shorter feedback loops and greater collaboration between technical and business functions as key benefits[2]. The study concluded that Agile helps organizations respond faster to external shifts by integrating learning cycles into their everyday operations.

Another cross-industry survey reported that seventy percent of organizations using Agile saw measurable improvements in decision-making and speed. The most significant gains appeared in sectors that extended Agile beyond IT into operations, finance, and customer service. These results indicate that Agile principles can support diverse business processes through transparency, rapid iteration, and team empowerment[3].

---

[1]Agile Business Consortium. 2022. "Agile Strategy | Agile Business Consortium." Agilebusiness.org. 2022.https://www.agilebusiness.org/business-agility/framework-for-business-agility/agile-strategy.html.

[2]Omonije, Ajibola . 2024. "Agile Methodology: A Comprehensive Impact on Modern Business Operations." ResearchGate.International Journal of Science and Research. February 6, 2024. https://www.researchgate.net/publication/377979833_Agile_Methodology_A_Comprehensive_Impact_on_Modern_Business_Operations.

[3]Celestin, Mbonigaba, S Sujatha, A Dinesh Kumar, and M Vasuki. 2024. "THE RISE of AGILE METHODOLOGIES in MANAGING COMPLEX BUSINESS PROJECTS: ENHANCING EFFICIENCY,..." ResearchGate 9 (2): 69–77. https://doi.org/10.5281/zenodo.13871832

In practice, industries that rely on constant feedback have benefited the most. Financial institutions apply Agile to manage compliance updates, risk assessments, and digital product launches. Retail organizations use iterative planning to adjust inventory and marketing strategies based on live sales data. Both examples show that when feedback cycles are short and information flows freely, strategy becomes responsive instead of reactive.

The Evolution of Agile Thinking

The original Agile Manifesto introduced principles meant for software teams, yet its foundation—inspect, adapt, and collaborate—has proven universal. The same three pillars that guide Scrum teams—transparency, inspection, and adaptation—also describe how organizations can manage strategic uncertainty. Leaders who review assumptions frequently and act on real evidence build a system capable of continuous learning.

The Agile Business Consortium expands this view by describing strategy as a living framework shaped by experimentation. Their research stresses that strategic objectives should remain visible but flexible, encouraging teams to test ideas early, measure progress, and refine plans without losing direction. This mindset turns strategy into a continuous conversation between leadership and teams rather than a top-down command. It also increases psychological safety, since teams know that data and learning guide decisions rather than rigid expectations[4].

Many leadership teams are applying these principles to reframe success metrics. Instead of relying solely on quarterly financials, they track delivery predictability, customer satisfaction, and

[4]Agile Business Consortium, *Agile Strategy*, 2022.

innovation throughput. This balanced set of measures allows organizations to identify weak signals of change early and adjust course. Agile thus becomes a mechanism for informed strategy execution rather than a collection of delivery tools.

Why Agile Is a Strategic Capability, Not a Toolkit

Agile creates value when it functions as a learning system across the enterprise. Feedback loops, retrospectives, and short planning horizons enable organizations to make evidence-based adjustments. Each iteration produces insight that guides the next investment or initiative. The Agile Business Consortium illustrates this relationship through a continuous loop connecting strategy, execution, and adaptation. When these three elements operate together, businesses maintain direction even as circumstances change.

The leadership role in such an environment is to facilitate learning rather than enforce compliance. Agile supports this by encouraging incremental planning, open communication, and cross-functional teamwork. Each sprint, release, or cycle becomes an opportunity to validate assumptions. Over time, the organization learns how to anticipate disruption rather than simply respond to it.

A useful way to visualize Agile's strategic function is through a comparison of traditional and iterative planning models:

Dimension	Traditional Planning	Agile Strategic Cycle
Planning horizon	Annual or multi-year	Continuous review
Decision triggers	Scheduled reporting	Real-time feedback
Control mechanism	Forecast accuracy	Learning and adaptation
Focus of teams	Delivery of fixed scope	Achievement of evolving outcomes
Leadership role	Directive	Coaching and facilitative

This structure transforms the organization into a network of small decision-making units that feed insight upward and across. When strategy evolves alongside delivery, innovation accelerates naturally.

Business leaders increasingly view Agile as a central capability because it links execution speed with strategic awareness. The approach creates a transparent environment where teams, product owners, and executives share responsibility for outcomes. It also enables organizations to manage uncertainty without sacrificing discipline—decisions are based on measurable learning rather than intuition.

As enterprises continue to navigate remote work, automation, and rapid technological shifts, those that use Agile as a strategic compass will find themselves better prepared to adapt. The following sections will explore how this adaptability drives innovation, customer value, and measurable business impact.

How Agile Drives Adaptability, Innovation, and Customer Value

Agile has proven that flexibility and focus can coexist in complex organizations. When understood deeply, its principles enable rapid learning and consistent alignment with what customers value most. Adaptability, innovation, and value delivery form the foundation of this strength. Each depends on how teams interpret and apply Agile's empirical approach: working transparently, inspecting results frequently, and adapting based on what they discover.

Adaptability Through Empirical Process Control

The ability to adapt quickly is one of the strongest outcomes of an Agile culture. According to experts, the pillars of transparency, inspection, and adaptation create a system where change becomes an informed decision rather than a disruption. Transparency allows everyone—from developers to executives—to see the real state of work. Inspection ensures that results are evaluated regularly and objectively. Adaptation provides the structure for responding to insights with measurable adjustments.

Agile organizations view change as part of their process, not an exception. This perspective is especially relevant for industries that face unpredictable market conditions. By using iterative planning, leaders can review short-term outcomes and decide whether to continue, redirect, or stop an initiative. This keeps strategic focus intact while allowing for course corrections.

Sprint reviews serve as a practical mechanism for this adaptability. They give teams and stakeholders a consistent opportunity to evaluate progress and market relevance. When treated as strategic checkpoints, these reviews allow decision-makers to assess business impact in real time. For instance, a product team can use a sprint review to present customer feedback, technical insights, and early performance data to leadership. That discussion often leads to informed changes in backlog priorities, preventing wasteful investment in low-value features.

The Scrum Master plays a critical role in this environment. They help the team interpret data objectively and facilitate communication between technical contributors and business leaders. By doing so, they maintain visibility on emerging risks and ensure that learning drives action. This combination of structured review and open dialogue allows organizations to stay aligned even as conditions shift.

Agile's adaptability also extends to risk management. Because teams inspect outcomes frequently, issues surface earlier and require less effort to resolve. A study of cross-functional Agile teams found that those using iterative inspection methods identified and mitigated project risks up to 40% faster than teams following traditional cycles[5].

This form of agility does not rely on reacting to change impulsively. It depends on disciplined observation, continuous learning, and leadership that supports experimentation without losing sight of goals.

Innovation Through Short Feedback Cycles

Agile's iterative rhythm creates the right conditions for innovation. Frequent feedback allows teams to test ideas quickly, evaluate customer response, and adjust direction before large

---

[5]AjibolaOmonije,*Int. J. of Science and Research*, 2024.

resources are committed. The shorter the feedback loop, the faster an organization can discover what truly works.

Atlassian highlights how connecting business strategy with development requires structured feedback channels between customers, teams, and executives. When insights flow easily, ideas move from concept to validation faster. Teams that integrate customer input into every sprint learn how to refine solutions while keeping product-market fit in constant view[6].

Innovation thrives when feedback is immediate and judgment-free. Agile rituals like retrospectives and reviews foster that climate. They encourage open reflection on what succeeded and what should improve. When teams understand that failure is data, not defeat, they build creative confidence. Over time, this mindset encourages experimentation, the foundation of sustainable innovation.

Organizations that apply Agile beyond technology often use short cycles to test business hypotheses. Marketing departments, for example, now conduct campaign sprints, where messaging and visuals are tested on small audiences before full release. Operations teams use Agile planning to trial process changes before implementing them across departments. These practices reduce the cost of innovation and increase the likelihood of meaningful results.

A culture that rewards learning over perfection enables these gains. Leaders can reinforce this culture by modeling curiosity, sharing outcomes transparently, and acknowledging lessons from

---

[6]Atlassian.n.d. "Connecting Business Strategy to Development Reality."Atlassian.https://www.atlassian.com/agile/advantage/connect-business-strategy-to-development-reality.

both success and failure. The Scrum Master supports this through facilitation and coaching, helping teams translate experimentation into actionable improvements.

The result is an environment where innovation is consistent rather than accidental. Instead of large, infrequent breakthroughs, progress occurs through a steady stream of small discoveries. Each feedback cycle becomes a building block for better design, faster delivery, and higher customer satisfaction.

The following table summarizes how iterative feedback enhances innovation outcomes:

Element	Traditional Approach	Agile Approach
Idea validation	Post-launch review	Continuous validation during development
Learning speed	Slow, based on large data sets	Fast, based on direct feedback
Risk exposure	High due to delayed learning	Reduced through frequent inspection
Team behavior	Task-focused	Learning-focused
Outcome	Occasional breakthroughs	Continuous incremental innovation

Research also indicates that organizations using such iterative frameworks report up to 30% shorter time-to-market and higher employee engagement, both indicators of an innovative work environment[7].

This improvement goes beyond faster delivery schedules. Shorter time-to-market means that ideas reach customers sooner, allowing companies to learn directly from real-world usage instead of relying solely on forecasts. Each release provides insight that

---

[7] Celestin Mbonigaba et al., *ResearchGate*, 2024

shapes the next iteration, reducing uncertainty and keeping innovation grounded in actual demand.

Higher employee engagement reflects the same mechanism at work internally. When teams see their ideas implemented quickly and their feedback valued, motivation strengthens. Autonomy in decision-making and visible results give people a clearer sense of purpose. Together, these conditions create a workplace where experimentation feels productive and learning is continuous.

Customer Value as the Ultimate Measure of Success

Customer satisfaction is the truest indicator of Agile's effectiveness. The framework is built around the principle that value is defined by the customer, not by internal measures of output. Organizations that align their delivery efforts with customer needs achieve more sustainable growth.

Experts emphasize that Agile's structure keeps the customer at the center of every decision. Product backlogs, sprint goals, and definition-of-done criteria all trace back to delivering meaningful value. This orientation ensures that business goals remain grounded in user outcomes rather than production metrics.

Agile teams measure value through both qualitative and quantitative feedback. Metrics such as **Net Promoter Score (NPS)**, customer effort score, and retention rate can complement Agile metrics like velocity and lead time. When analyzed together, they reveal whether faster delivery also translates into real satisfaction. For example:

- A rising NPS indicates that product updates are improving the customer experience.
- A declining customer effort score signals smoother interactions or better usability.

13

- Stable or increasing retention rates confirm that iterative improvements are addressing user priorities.

Integrating these metrics helps leadership understand how daily delivery contributes to long-term value creation. It also provides teams with tangible evidence of impact, strengthening motivation and ownership.

A consistent feedback mechanism further enhances this relationship. Sprint reviews, customer demos, and user research sessions create opportunities to gather direct input and align priorities. Atlassian's framework for connecting strategy to delivery suggests involving customers or their representatives regularly in sprint outcomes to maintain visibility of value creation.

Customer value also benefits from cross-functional collaboration. When marketing, design, and development work together, they bring diverse perspectives to problem-solving. This integration minimizes rework and ensures that features or services meet expectations early in the process.

Research consistently shows that companies emphasizing customer-centered Agile practices outperform peers in satisfaction and loyalty measures. The approach does not rely on complex incentives or slogans—it works because the system itself is built to listen, learn, and adjust.

The Business Case for Scrum

Scrum has become one of the most widely adopted Agile frameworks because it delivers measurable business results. It gives organizations a structure for continuous delivery, faster response to market shifts, and better alignment between strategy and execution. The framework's principles—iteration, transparency, and accountability—link daily activities to larger business outcomes. This section explores three major ways Scrum creates value through:

- speed and responsiveness,
- continuous feedback and learning, and
- strategic alignment across roles.

Speed and Responsiveness

Organizations adopt Scrum because it accelerates delivery without sacrificing quality. The framework enables teams to deliver usable increments in short, predictable cycles, giving leaders the ability to assess progress and outcomes more frequently. According to industry data, organizations using Scrum report improved time-to-market, faster decision cycles, and greater adaptability to external changes.

Scrum's design naturally supports business responsiveness. The short sprint cadence allows teams to release partial value regularly, obtain feedback early, and make timely adjustments. Every sprint produces a working increment, meaning that potential revenue, cost savings, or learning can begin before a full project concludes. From a financial perspective, this reduces sunk costs and brings earlier returns on investment.

This model also enhances decision agility. Frequent checkpoints—planning sessions, daily standups, sprint reviews, and retrospectives—provide multiple opportunities to evaluate priorities and address bottlenecks. Leaders receive consistent visibility into progress, enabling better forecasting and risk management.

A study of global Agile teams found that Scrum organizations adjusted project direction up to 25% faster due to structured transparency mechanisms[8].Velocity, however, only has meaning when paired with predictability. Systems thinking emphasizes that sustainable speed emerges from stability and clear flow rather than constant acceleration. Scrum helps balance these two elements by creating rhythm. Time-boxed sprints, clear roles, and visible progress metrics allow teams to identify early signs of imbalance, such as overcommitment or recurring technical debt, and make incremental corrections before performance declines.

Scrum Masters play an enabling role in this balance. They monitor process flow, address impediments, and coach the team toward a sustainable pace. Their responsibility is to ensure that faster delivery never undermines quality or team morale. When managed well, this combination of structure and adaptability creates a cycle of steady improvement rather than fluctuating productivity spikes.

Continuous Feedback and Learning

Scrum's most valuable contribution to business success lies in its built-in learning system. Every sprint represents an opportunity to collect data, analyze performance, and improve. This empirical process helps teams base their actions on evidence rather than assumptions. The cadence of short cycles turns learning into a habit rather than a reactive task.

Scrum introduces formal inspection points, sprint reviews and retrospectives, that ensure consistent evaluation. Sprint reviews connect the team to stakeholders and customers, focusing on whether the increment delivers real value. Retrospectives focus internally, examining how collaboration, quality, and communication can improve. Both activities transform feedback into actionable insights.

---

[8] Celestin Mbonigaba et al., *ResearchGate*, 2024

When organizations treat these events as strategic learning sessions rather than administrative routines, they unlock significant efficiency gains. A multinational manufacturing company had integrated its sprint retrospectives into broader operational reviews.

By analyzing recurring defects and communication delays, it identified redundant approval steps in its production process. Simplifying those workflows reduced rework costs by 18% within two quarters. This outcome illustrates how small, disciplined adjustments in Scrum cycles can yield measurable financial impact.

Continuous learning also strengthens accountability. Teams that track metrics such as defect rates, cycle time, and throughput can clearly see the effects of their decisions. Over time, this visibility fosters intrinsic motivation. Employees understand how their actions influence business outcomes and take ownership of improvement.

Agile leaders emphasize that Scrum's learning loops extend beyond the team. When leadership reviews sprint outcomes alongside teams, insights travel upward, shaping future strategy. This two-way learning flow ensures that long-term planning reflects current realities. The Agile Business Consortium refers to this as "organizational learning agility"—the ability to adapt strategy in response to empirical evidence rather than static forecasts.

The benefits of continuous feedback become especially clear in complex environments where conditions evolve faster than plans can keep up. Frequent evaluation cycles prevent large-scale failure by surfacing small issues early. They also enable experimentation, allowing teams to test ideas on a limited scale before wider deployment.

The following table summarizes how Scrum's learning cycle enhances decision-making:

Scrum Mechanism	Primary Function	Business Outcome
Sprint Planning	Define goals and priorities	Clear focus, reduced waste
Daily Scrum	Inspect daily progress	Early detection of risks
Sprint Review	Collect stakeholder feedback	Improved alignment and relevance
Retrospective	Identify process improvements	Continuous efficiency gains

This structured rhythm of inspection and adaptation replaces long, inflexible project cycles with an ongoing dialogue between delivery and value. It also gives organizations a reliable structure for experimentation, something traditional planning models rarely support.

Strategic Alignment Across Roles

While speed and learning are valuable on their own, their true business impact appears when all roles in Scrum work toward shared objectives. Scrum creates this alignment by defining clear accountabilities: the Product Owner represents value, the Scrum Master ensures flow and process effectiveness, and the Development Team delivers increments that meet agreed standards. Together, these roles create a transparent system where business goals and execution remain synchronized.

This alignment is crucial in large or distributed organizations, where communication gaps can easily lead to misdirection and confusion. Scrum provides a framework for visibility across functions. Backlog refinement, sprint reviews, and transparent task boards ensure that every contributor understands how their work connects to overall priorities. When leadership uses these same tools for decision-making, strategy remains visible at every level.

Scrum.org emphasizes that the Scrum Master is accountable for ensuring delivery effectiveness. By removing barriers, coaching teams, and supporting the Product Owner, they connect operational performance to strategic intent. This role often serves as a bridge between business leaders seeking results and teams focused on execution. Through this facilitation, organizations maintain coherence without reverting to top-down control.

Effective backlog refinement further strengthens this connection. During refinement, teams clarify upcoming priorities with the Product Owner and verify that backlog items reflect business outcomes rather than task lists. This process ensures that each sprint contributes measurable value. When performed consistently, refinement transforms the backlog into a living artifact of organizational strategy rather than a static task repository.

Strategic alignment also depends on how information flows between leadership and teams. Regular engagement in sprint reviews allows executives to validate assumptions and witness progress directly. This transparency reduces misinterpretation and shortens the decision-making cycle. It also builds trust, as teams see leadership engaged in understanding the real challenges of delivery.

Organizations that embed Scrum across multiple teams often adopt coordination practices such as Scrum of Scrums or scaled Agile frameworks. These practices extend alignment across departments while preserving autonomy within teams. The key principle remains the same: strategy must flow downward in clear priorities, while learning flows upward to inform future direction.

In enterprises that manage portfolios of initiatives, alignment metrics can include delivery predictability, business value realized, and stakeholder satisfaction. These measures connect the rhythm of Scrum teams to financial and operational results. Over time, organizations learn to manage dependencies and investments through transparent metrics rather than command structures.

The relationship between the Product Owner, Scrum Master, and Team forms a compact that ensures accountability at every level. The table below summarizes their shared alignment responsibilities:

Role	Primary Focus	Contribution to Alignment
Product Owner	Customer and business value	Defines and prioritizes outcomes
Scrum Master	Process and delivery health	Ensures flow, removes impediments
Development Team	Product creation	Delivers increments that meet expectations
Leadership	Strategic oversight	Integrates team insights into business direction

When these responsibilities work together, the organization develops a unified rhythm. Each sprint aligns effort, evidence, and strategic priorities tangibly. The outcome is not only consistent delivery but a culture of shared purpose.

Thus, Scrum's business impact is grounded in three interconnected capabilities: delivering faster with control, learning continuously through feedback, and maintaining alignment across roles. Together, these qualities allow organizations to transform agility into a measurable competitive advantage.

Speed without chaos, learning without waste, and coordination without hierarchy are the conditions Scrum creates when practiced with intent. Besides optimizing workflow, this framework builds a system where every iteration contributes to business performance.

Common Misconceptions That Limit Agile's Impact

Agile continues to grow in popularity, yet many organizations still misunderstand its principles and intent. Misinterpretation often leads to partial implementation or misplaced expectations, reducing the benefits that Agile and Scrum can deliver. The most persistent misconceptions involve structure, scope, and strategy. Each one restricts progress by distorting what Agile was designed to achieve.

Misconception 1: Agile Equals Lack of Structure

A common belief is that Agile encourages disorder or a free-form approach to work. In reality, Agile frameworks are built on clearly defined principles that ensure accountability and transparency. Scrum, for instance, operates through an empirical process based on three core pillars: transparency, inspection, and adaptation. These elements create a structure that promotes learning and control, not chaos.

Each Scrum event has a specific purpose. Sprint planning sets clear goals, the daily Scrum keeps progress visible, and retrospectives drive measurable improvement. The defined time boxes, roles, and deliverables prevent drift and maintain focus. The flexibility lies in how teams adapt within those boundaries, not in the absence of them.

Self-organization, another misunderstood term, does not mean teams operate without oversight. It means they take ownership of achieving agreed objectives. This model increases accountability because outcomes are owned by those directly involved in the work. When teams self-organize effectively, decision-making becomes faster, and responsibility for quality becomes shared across roles.

The Scrum Master ensures that this balance between structure and freedom remains healthy. As explained by experts, the Scrum Master acts as a leader who supports discipline through empowerment. They guide adherence to Scrum rules while enabling teams to experiment and improve processes. The role demonstrates that structure and autonomy can coexist when guided by principles and supported by trust.

When leaders misunderstand Agile as unstructured, they risk removing the very mechanisms that make it effective. Structure is what makes adaptation possible. Without it, there is no reliable framework for learning or improvement.

Misconception 2: Agile Is Only for IT or Software

Another misconception is that Agile applies only to software development. While Agile originated in technology, its principles have proven relevant to nearly every business function. Many organizations in finance, healthcare, marketing, and human resources now use Agile to increase responsiveness and collaboration.

In finance, teams apply iterative planning for compliance projects and digital transformation efforts. By working in short cycles and testing frequently, financial institutions manage regulatory updates more efficiently and reduce project risks. Healthcare organizations have adopted Agile to streamline patient-care systems, manage research programs, and improve data workflows. Marketing teams use Agile to launch campaigns in short iterations, review audience feedback, and refine messages continuously. Human resources departments run recruitment and performance initiatives through Agile cycles to improve transparency and employee engagement.

The shared outcome in all these examples is improved adaptability. Agile's iterative approach allows teams to assess progress frequently and adjust to changing requirements or market signals. The framework's emphasis on collaboration and inspection helps cross-functional teams coordinate their efforts and align decisions quickly.

Research supports this cross-industry adaptability. Studies on Agile adoption across sectors show consistent benefits in communication, productivity, and stakeholder alignment. Organizations that adopt Agile outside IT report higher satisfaction among internal clients, faster resolution of dependencies, and greater visibility into project goals.

The following table highlights examples of Agile applications beyond IT:

Industry	Agile Application	Outcome
Finance	Iterative compliance and reporting processes	Faster risk assessment and audit readiness
Healthcare	Managing clinical projects and patient data	Improved coordination and response time
Marketing	Campaign sprints and A/B testing	Rapid audience insight and content refinement
Human Resources	Recruitment and training cycles	Higher engagement and shorter hiring timelines

Misconception 3: Agile Is Incompatible with Strategic Planning

A third misunderstanding is that Agile cannot coexist with a long-term strategy. This misconception stems from viewing planning as a one-time event instead of an evolving process. In reality,

Agile offers an alternative model of strategic management—one that replaces rigid timelines with continuous alignment between vision and action.

Research defines strategy as an iterative framework guided by short, evidence-based cycles. Plans are reviewed frequently, using real data from ongoing initiatives to validate or adjust direction. This approach connects long-term goals with immediate feedback, ensuring the strategy remains relevant in fast-changing environments.

Agile organizations treat every iteration as a small-scale experiment that informs the next decision. Rather than discarding long-term objectives, they use shorter cycles to move toward them more effectively. This mindset reduces waste by testing ideas early, identifying weak assumptions, and prioritizing investments with the highest impact.

Leaders play a central role in making this iterative strategy work. They create conditions for teams to deliver continuous insight into market trends, customer needs, and operational performance. When leadership reviews sprint outcomes or quarterly increments, they gain real-time visibility into whether strategy and execution remain aligned.

Agile leaders act as facilitators of learning rather than enforcers of plans. They focus on maintaining clarity of purpose while empowering teams to adapt and deliver that purpose. In this environment, planning and execution merge into a single cycle of exploration, validation, and refinement.

Organizations that adopt this approach gain flexibility without losing direction. They build resilience by ensuring that decisions are guided by evidence, not assumption. Over time, this adaptability becomes a strategic advantage.

Agile as a Foundation for Business Agility

Agile has grown from a project management framework into a core operating philosophy for modern organizations. Its principles—transparency, collaboration, and iteration—form the groundwork for business agility, where companies learn continuously and adapt deliberately. When practiced beyond teams, Agile becomes the foundation for enterprise growth and strategic coherence.

Integrating Agile with Business Strategy

Enterprise agility begins when strategic planning and Agile delivery operate as a single system. This integration is defined as a loop where strategy is created, tested, and refined through ongoing feedback. Objectives and Key Results (OKRs) become the link between company vision and team outcomes. Short review cycles ensure that investment decisions reflect current data rather than assumptions.

Agile aligns naturally with portfolio and program management. Atlassian explains that connecting business goals to development reality requires visibility across all levels of work. Dashboards, sprint metrics, and customer feedback reveal how each initiative contributes to strategic value. This transparency allows leadership to evaluate trade-offs and redirect priorities before risks escalate.

When organizations expand Agile principles beyond product teams, they move from incremental improvement to enterprise transformation. Finance, human resources, and operations adopt iterative planning, learning to deliver value through cycles of experimentation. The outcome is faster adaptation to market signals and a clearer understanding of how every department supports shared objectives.

Scrum provides the rhythm for this alignment. Its defined cadence—planning, execution, review, and reflection—creates predictable opportunities for learning. Each sprint serves as a mini strategic experiment where outcomes are measured, feedback is collected, and insights are applied. Over time, this rhythm ensures that business direction remains responsive while staying connected to long-term goals.

Building an Organization That Learns and Adapts

A truly Agile organization is one that learns faster than its environment changes. Continuous improvement, built into Agile through retrospectives and empirical inspection, keeps learning at the center of operations. The key is consistency. Teams and leaders must treat every project as an opportunity to refine systems and strengthen collaboration.

Scrum Masters and Agile leaders sustain this learning culture. They coach teams to recognize patterns, identify systemic issues, and respond with small, measurable adjustments. Their focus on process health, feedback flow, and team morale helps preserve psychological safety—an essential condition for creativity and accountability. When people feel safe to question and experiment, innovation becomes part of daily work rather than a rare event.

Business agility also depends on how well leadership models adaptability. Executives who use empirical data to adjust priorities send a clear message that flexibility is a strength. This mindset reinforces trust across layers of the organization, reducing resistance to change. Over time, the company's structure itself evolves toward autonomy supported by alignment—teams are empowered to act while guided by shared purpose.

As Agile matures, it becomes less about adopting ceremonies and more about cultivating a shared way of thinking. Organizations that succeed treat feedback as a strategic resource, linking learning directly to performance. They build systems that adapt naturally, making improvement continuous and sustainable.

Chapter 2: The Scrum Master's True Mandate

In today's Agile-driven organizations, the role of the Scrum Master continues to evolve. This chapter explores the breadth of what the Scrum Master is truly meant to deliver—beyond ceremonies and checklists. We'll examine how servant leadership and strategic facilitation coexist, how the Scrum Master acts as a systems thinker and team coach, and which outcomes matter most: velocity, predictability, and team health. Along the way, we'll review practical stances, decision points, and behaviors that elevate the role into a strategic partner for the business.

The Leadership Spectrum – Servant Leadership and Strategic Facilitation

Defining Servant Leadership in the Scrum Context

Servant leadership in Scrum places team needs first, removes friction, and cultivates conditions where people can do their best work. The Scrum Master serves through coaching, facilitation, and impediment removal, while protecting time for focus and learning. This service is active. It involves sensing where the team struggles, making issues visible, and building capability so the team resolves more on its own over time. The standard is empowerment with accountability, not passive support[9].

The tension practitioners feel is real. A Scrum Master who only serves may leave systemic blockers untouched. A Scrum Master who only directs may suppress initiative. The craft sits between these extremes: enable self-management, escalate when necessary, and keep the system transparent so decisions rest on evidence rather than opinion. Practical signs of healthy servant leadership include clear Sprint Goals, visible work in progress, rapid help on blockers, and regular improvement experiments that actually reach "done."

Situations call for movement across the spectrum. When the team is new to Scrum, the Scrum Master often teaches the basics and facilitates events closely. When the team gains fluency, the Scrum Master shifts toward coaching and stewardship of flow. When outside constraints stall delivery, the Scrum Master broadens the radius of action to involve stakeholders, negotiate dependencies, and remove organizational impediments that the team cannot address alone[10].

Two safeguards keep servant leadership from becoming vague. First, keep outcomes visible: flow metrics, quality signals, and Sprint Goal attainment. Second, keep agreements explicit: Definition of Done, entry and exit criteria, and a clear backlog

---

[9]Overeem, Barry. 2022. "The 6 Stances of a Scrum Master - the Liberators - Medium." Medium.The Liberators. March 14, 2022. https://medium.com/the-liberators/the-6-stances-of-a-scrum-master-a0f0666b95.

[10]Leffingwell, Dean. 2014. "Scrum Master/Team Coach." Scaled Agile Framework. July 24, 2014. https://framework.scaledagile.com/scrum-master-team-coach.

refinement rhythm. Service then has an operational edge. It can be inspected and improved like any other part of the system[11].

Strategic Facilitation as a Leadership Act

Strategic facilitation aligns daily activity with business intent. The Scrum Master helps the Product Owner and team translate goals into a focused backlog, exposes tradeoffs early, and creates space for evidence to shape choices. The emphasis is on clarity and cadence, so decisions move forward without endless rework[12].

Facilitative behaviors that raise business confidence:

- **Map backlog items** to explicit outcomes or OKRs so priority signals are unambiguous.

- **Prepare Sprint Reviews** with a storyline that ties increments to customer impact and next bets.

- **Bring the right voices** into the room at the right time, then run a purposeful conversation that ends with a decision and an owner.

- **Keep visual controls current**: forecast ranges, cumulative flow, and risk lists that are short and acted on.

- **Escalate impediments with context and options**, not complaints.

Good facilitation is also situational. When dialogue stalls, the Scrum Master uses structures that balance participation and decision speed. Examples include timeboxed option generation,

---

[11]Sa, Erika. n.d. "Scrum Metrics."Atlassian.https://www.atlassian.com/agile/scrum/scrum-metrics.
[12]Dean Leffingwell,*Scaled Agile Framework*, 2014.

decider protocols, and explicit "try for one Sprint" experiments. The goal is movement with learning, not perfect consensus. Over time, this rhythm reduces decision latency and restores trust between delivery teams and stakeholders[13].

Strategic facilitation is compatible with servant leadership because it protects autonomy while connecting effort to outcomes the organization values. It respects expertise in the team and still insists that progress, risks, and results remain visible to sponsors. This balance is what gives the role influence beyond ceremonies.

Choosing the Stance That Matches Context

Experienced Scrum Masters work with a palette of stances. Common ones include teacher, coach, facilitator, mentor, impediment remover, and change agent. Each comes with distinct behaviors and risks if overused. The discipline is to select deliberately, not reflexively.

A simple decision frame helps:

- **If knowledge is the gap**, teach the minimum needed to unblock the next step. Keep it interactive and tied to current work.

- **If insight is the gap**, coach with questions that surface assumptions and options the team already holds.

- **If coordination is   the gap**, facilitate the conversation that gets the right people to a clear decision.

- **If the system is the gap**, act as an impediment remover or change agent and engage leaders to fix cross-team or policy constraints.

---

[13]Barry Overeem, *The Liberators* (Medium, 2022).

Three quick questions to ask before choosing a stance:

1. *What is blocking progress right now: skill, clarity, decision, or constraint?*
2. *Who owns the next move: the team, the Product Owner, or someone outside the team?*
3. *What evidence will show this worked within one Sprint?*

Stance selection also benefits from lightweight diagnostics. Review the Sprint Goal reliability, carryover ratio, and the age of work in progress. If Sprint Goals regularly slip due to missing decisions, lean into facilitation and stakeholder engagement. If quality issues recur, emphasize teaching around the Definition of Done and fast feedback on defects. If external dependencies dominate, take the change agent stance and negotiate policy adjustments or service-level expectations with adjacent groups.

Finally, stance switching is a signal in itself. Explain to the team why you are taking a different posture this week and what result you expect. Close the loop in the Retrospective by checking whether the switch helped. This keeps the role transparent and models empirical leadership.

The Scrum Master as Systems Thinker and Team Coach

Systems Thinking: Viewing the Team as Part of a Wider System

A Scrum Master sees the team as one element in a network of interdependent systems—product development, operations, customer feedback, and corporate governance. Every delay, hand-off, or unclear dependency reveals how these systems interact. Systems thinking helps identify patterns beneath surface symptoms. For example, recurring missed sprint goals may stem from unclear product ownership or external approvals, not from team capability. Understanding those feedback loops enables the Scrum Master to intervene where it matters most[14].

Key questions guide this perspective:

- Where are queues forming between teams or departments?

- Which policies, rather than people, are producing recurring delays?

- What data sources—support tickets, release metrics, customer comments—reflect systemic friction?

By mapping these interactions, the Scrum Master supports decisions that improve the entire value stream instead of only team velocity. This approach aligns with modern Agile governance, which values flow efficiency over local optimization[15].

Systems thinking also exposes hidden feedback delays. When information moves slowly between customers and delivery, learning decays. By shortening these loops—through sprint reviews, telemetry dashboards, or shared metrics—the Scrum Master ensures that insight travels as fast as output. It turns Agile's inspect-and-adapt principle into a company-wide feedback mechanism.

Coaching the Team Toward Self-Organization and High Performance

Coaching remains one of the Scrum Master's most visible responsibilities. Coaching here means enabling people to see

---

[14]Dean Leffingwell,*Scaled Agile Framework*, 2014.

[15]Erika Sa, *Atlassian*, n.d.

issues clearly and find their own solutions, rather than providing answers. Experts emphasize three practical behaviors:

- Ask powerful questions. Instead of giving advice, prompt reflection: What options have we not considered? What evidence supports this decision?

- Encourage learning through small experiments. Use short feedback cycles so the team can observe impact and adjust quickly.

- Promote accountability through shared commitments. Guide the team to set realistic sprint goals and inspect progress daily.

Effective coaching develops both competence and confidence. As skills strengthen, teams manage risk and dependencies more autonomously. The Scrum Master gradually reduces directive facilitation, focusing instead on maintaining psychological safety—a state where team members can raise problems without fear of blame.

Psychological safety directly influences performance. Research cited in Agile leadership studies links it to innovation and sustained delivery. Scrum events provide natural checkpoints to reinforce it: retrospectives for honest reflection, sprint planning for collaborative goal-setting, and reviews for transparent feedback. The Scrum Master shapes these environments by modelling curiosity, acknowledging mistakes, and treating feedback as data, not judgment[16].

---

[16]SandhyaDevarinti. 2021. "Scrum Masters Are True Leaders Who Serve the Scrum Team and the Larger Organization. The Servant as a Leader: The Servant-Leader Is Servant First." Linkedin.com. June 8, 2021. https://www.linkedin.com/pulse/scrum-master-leader-servantship-servant-leadership-sandhya-reddy/.

Collaboration health is another dimension of coaching. When communication falters, the Scrum Master helps clarify interfaces between roles. Regular check-ins with the Product Owner maintain a balance between delivery capacity and business demand. With other teams, alignment meetings and clear definitions of "done" minimize misunderstandings. A well-coached team doesn't depend on constant supervision; it manages commitments with confidence and corrects course quickly when needed.

The shift toward high performance also requires attention to morale and workload. The Scrum Master observes team energy, highlights unsustainable pace, and facilitates workload adjustments before burnout occurs. Short surveys or informal temperature checks after retrospectives can reveal early signs of stress. Over time, maintaining a stable pace becomes both a cultural norm and a productivity advantage.

Balancing Process Improvement and Delivery Flow

Continuous improvement is central to Agile, yet improvement efforts that interrupt delivery can erode trust. The Scrum Master's challenge is to balance learning with throughput. Data-driven metrics help maintain this balance.

Useful flow indicators include:

- **Cycle time** – how long work takes from start to finish.
- **Throughput** – how many items are completed in a period.
- **Work-in-progress (WIP)** – how many tasks are underway at once.

Monitoring these measures provides early warning of bottlenecks without turning performance into a contest.

The Scrum Master guides the team to interpret these metrics constructively. A rising cycle time may indicate overloaded work queues or unplanned rework. Rather than enforcing arbitrary targets, the Scrum Master facilitates inquiry: What's slowing us down? Which step adds the least value? This keeps metrics as tools for insight rather than pressure.

Improvement initiatives should fit within the delivery rhythm. Many high-performing teams allocate a small capacity percentage each sprint for experiments—process tweaks, automation trials, or skill development. This approach embeds learning in the system instead of treating it as extra work. The Scrum Master coordinates these experiments and ensures results are reviewed publicly, so learning compounds rather than disappears.

Recognizing impediments early is equally vital. Some are visible—technical debt, unclear requirements—while others are systemic, like conflicting departmental goals. The Scrum Master documents and categorizes impediments, escalating those that exceed team influence. This evidence-based escalation turns impediment removal into an organizational learning process.

Fostering a culture of learning means closing the loop on every improvement. The Scrum Master encourages teams to record what was tried, what changed, and what outcomes followed. Over several sprints, these logs form a history of cause-and-effect that informs future experiments. Leaders value this because it demonstrates progress grounded in data, not slogans.

Ultimately, balancing improvement and delivery flow transforms Agile from a project method into an operational discipline. Teams deliver predictably while refining their own system. The Scrum Master's quiet success lies in making this balance self-sustaining—teams that learn continuously, improve incrementally, and maintain momentum across changing contexts.

Key Outcomes the Scrum Master Should Own – Velocity, Predictability, Team Health

The effectiveness of a Scrum Master cannot be assessed by activity alone; it is reflected in the outcomes that demonstrate a healthy, high-performing system. Velocity, predictability, and team health form the core of these outcomes. Together, they shape an organization's confidence in Agile delivery and its ability to sustain value creation over time. The Scrum Master acts as the steward of these results, guiding teams toward continuous improvement through clarity, evidence, and trust.

Velocity: What It Represents and How to Interpret It

Velocity is one of the most commonly tracked Scrum metrics, yet it is also one of the most misunderstood. It measures the amount of work a team completes in a sprint, typically expressed in story points. Used properly, it helps teams forecast their commitments and provides a baseline for future planning. The purpose of velocity is not to measure individual performance but to help the team understand its delivery capacity over time[17].

Velocity trends matter more than single values. A consistent or gradually improving velocity suggests stable team performance and predictable delivery. Large fluctuations often indicate systemic issues, such as inconsistent backlog refinement, unclear sprint goals, or external interruptions. A Scrum Master observing

---

[17]Erika Sa, *Atlassian*, n.d.

these trends helps the team explore causes through retrospectives, encouraging evidence-based adjustments rather than arbitrary pressure.

Misuse of velocity can damage trust and motivation. When teams are compared based on velocity or judged for producing lower numbers, they tend to inflate story points or focus on quantity over quality. Experts emphasize that velocity should never be a competitive benchmark between teams because each team's estimation scale is unique. Instead, velocity works best as a local learning metric—useful for the team to improve flow, manage commitments, and identify bottlenecks.

To ensure velocity drives the right behavior, the Scrum Master promotes transparency around its purpose. During sprint reviews, they highlight how velocity trends relate to real outcomes—business value delivered, quality maintained, or risks reduced. This keeps the metric in context and ensures stakeholders focus on impact rather than output.

Key principles for meaningful velocity tracking:

- Maintain consistency in team estimations and avoid cross-team comparisons.
- Use at least three sprints of data before drawing conclusions.
- Discuss changes in velocity through retrospectives, not executive dashboards.
- Correlate velocity trends with other indicators, such as cycle time and sprint goal success rate, for a full picture of delivery health.

Predictability: Planning Reliability and Business Confidence

Predictability measures the team's ability to deliver on what it commits to within a sprint or release. High predictability builds confidence among stakeholders because it demonstrates reliability and a commitment to discipline. The Scrum Master plays a central role in helping the team achieve this consistency through cadence, data, and transparent communication.

Tools such as burndown charts, cumulative flow diagrams, and lead time metrics provide visibility into how predictably work moves through the system. A burndown chart displays the rate at which tasks are completed in relation to the sprint goal, indicating whether progress aligns with expectations. Cumulative flow diagrams expose bottlenecks by visualizing work in its various states—planned, in progress, and completed. Lead time measures the duration from task initiation to completion, indicating process efficiency.

When used together, these metrics indicate whether the team is consistently delivering value or facing systemic challenges. For example, widening bands in a cumulative flow diagram may signal overcommitment or delays in testing. The Scrum Master facilitates discussions on these insights, guiding the team to adjust the scope, balance the workload, or refine the acceptance criteria before problems escalate.

Predictability also depends on clear sprint planning. A Scrum Master ensures that planning includes not only workload estimation but also risk assessment and capacity considerations. Teams that plan collaboratively, accounting for both expected and potential interruptions, tend to deliver closer to their commitments. Over time, this creates a rhythm where stakeholders can rely on sprint outcomes as a dependable part of business forecasting.

An important part of predictability is communication. The Scrum Master promotes transparency by making data visible to all stakeholders, including team members, product owners, and business sponsors. When commitments are at risk, the focus is on solutions and learning, not blame. This openness transforms metrics from control tools into trust-building mechanisms, reinforcing Agile's emphasis on shared ownership of outcomes.

Predictability, when maintained, contributes directly to business performance. Reliable delivery enables more accurate budget planning, smoother product launches, and higher confidence in release timelines. It shifts leadership focus from firefighting to strategic investment.

Team Health: The Less Visible but Critical Outcome

Team health underpins every measurable output. Without a healthy team, velocity and predictability become temporary gains that quickly erode under stress. The Scrum Master is the guardian of this foundation, ensuring that collaboration, communication, and psychological safety remain intact as delivery pressures increase.

Indicators of team health include:

- Consistent participation in events with constructive dialogue.
- Balance between focus and flexibility in handling change.
- Evidence of shared ownership, where issues are raised early and solved collectively.

- Sustainable pace reflected in low turnover and stable morale[18].

Regular retrospectives provide a structured approach to evaluating these indicators. The Scrum Master encourages open conversation by modelling honesty and active listening. When tensions arise, they facilitate discussions that separate problems from people, preserving respect while addressing root causes. Feedback loops extend beyond retrospectives; casual check-ins and one-on-one sessions help the Scrum Master sense early warning signs such as fatigue or disengagement.

Psychological safety is particularly important. It allows innovation and accountability to coexist. Teams that feel safe challenging assumptions and experimenting with new approaches tend to discover better solutions faster. Research on Agile performance reveals that psychological safety is strongly correlated with adaptability and product quality. The Scrum Master fosters this by reinforcing the idea that mistakes are opportunities for learning, not judgment.

Maintaining team health also involves attention to balance. Continuous delivery without recovery time leads to burnout. The Scrum Master monitors workload distribution and reminds leadership when unrealistic expectations threaten sustainability. Over multiple sprints, this advocacy stabilizes performance and preserves trust between the team and the organization.

Beyond well-being, healthy teams exhibit resilience. They recover from setbacks quickly, maintain focus during change, and continuously refine how they work together. The Scrum Master's

---

[18]SandhyaDevarinti, "Scrum Masters Are True Leaders Who Serve the Scrum Team and the Larger Organization," *LinkedIn*, 2021.

consistent presence and steady communication reinforce this stability, even in uncertainty.

Connecting These Outcomes to Business Value

Velocity, predictability, and team health are not isolated metrics— they converge to define organizational agility. Together they determine whether Agile practices translate into measurable business benefits.

Improved velocity supports faster time-to-market, allowing companies to release value earlier and gather real customer feedback sooner. Predictability reduces financial and operational risk by making delivery timelines credible. Strong team health sustains innovation and minimizes turnover, which lowers recruitment and onboarding costs. When tracked together, these outcomes reveal the maturity of an organization's Agile system.

The Scrum Master connects these metrics to strategic objectives by presenting them as indicators of value flow rather than productivity. For instance:

- Stable velocity with high sprint goal success signals delivery consistency.

- Predictable lead times show efficiency in responding to market shifts.

- Positive team engagement surveys indicate cultural resilience during scaling efforts.

A simple example of this connection can be shown through a summary table:

Outcome	Scrum Metrics	Business Impact
Velocity	Story points per sprint	Faster time-to-market and early ROI

Outcome	Scrum Metrics	Business Impact
Predictability	Burndown charts, cumulative flow, lead time	Reliable delivery and stakeholder confidence
Team Health	Engagement, retention, psychological safety indicators	Sustainable innovation and reduced attrition

The Scrum Master's accountability extends beyond reporting these numbers. Their role is to interpret what the data implies for the organization and initiate conversations that drive systemic change. For example, if predictability drops despite steady velocity, the Scrum Master investigates external dependencies or planning habits. If velocity improves while team morale declines, they explore whether work pressure has exceeded sustainable limits. This diagnostic capability turns metrics into actionable insights.

Even though Scrum Masters cannot control all variables—such as shifting business priorities or resource constraints—they influence the conditions that determine success. They build feedback systems, facilitate honest dialogue, and protect the environment, allowing continuous improvement to flourish. Over time, these behaviors create an organizational habit of using data to learn rather than to punish, resulting in a culture that values progress supported by evidence.

A Scrum Master's real contribution is measured in outcomes that endure beyond individual sprints. By guiding teams toward balanced velocity, reliable predictability, and resilient team health, they transform Agile metrics into strategic assets. These outcomes reflect not only the performance of a team but also the strength of the organization's learning system—where data informs improvement, trust sustains delivery, and adaptability becomes an integral part of the business identity.

The Scrum Master's Mandate in Action – Navigating Complexity and Scaling Influence

Adapting the Mandate in Distributed, Hybrid, and Scaled Environments

Modern Agile work increasingly takes place across distributed and hybrid setups, where coordination and visibility become more challenging. The Scrum Master's role in such contexts extends beyond facilitating ceremonies; it includes designing systems that sustain engagement, clarity, and collaboration despite distance.

In hybrid environments, the Scrum Master relies on digital facilitation tools to recreate the shared understanding that co-located teams achieve through physical proximity. Visual boards, asynchronous stand-ups, and virtual retrospectives help maintain transparency and rhythm. The key is not the tool itself but how it enables shared ownership—every member should see the same progress, impediments, and outcomes at any time.

Time zone differences require new patterns of communication. Asynchronous updates, recorded sprint reviews, and documented decisions reduce dependency on overlapping hours. The Scrum Master models this behavior, ensuring decisions are logged, discussions are visible, and no member feels excluded. Consistency of information becomes a substitute for physical presence.

When multiple teams work toward a shared goal, coordination frameworks such as Scrum of Scrums or scaled Agile models help synchronize progress. The Scrum Master facilitates these cross-team forums by focusing on flow dependencies, risk visibility, and alignment of release goals. Effective coordination ensures that local optimization does not undermine the broader delivery system.

In scaled contexts, the Scrum Master also acts as a bridge between program-level management and delivery teams. They help leadership interpret team metrics correctly, highlighting systemic constraints rather than individual performance issues. This transparency strengthens trust between delivery and governance, allowing faster and more informed decisions.

Influencing Beyond the Team: Stakeholder, Product Owner, and Business Engagement

The Scrum Master's influence reaches far beyond the development team. Their ability to coach stakeholders and facilitate meaningful engagement determines how effectively Agile principles take root across the organization.

One of the most critical relationships is with the Product Owner. The Scrum Master supports the Product Owner in managing the backlog strategically—prioritizing based on value rather than urgency. They facilitate refinement sessions where items are clarified, ordered, and connected to measurable outcomes. This partnership ensures that the product vision translates into actionable increments that reflect customer needs and business strategy.

Engaging stakeholders is equally vital. The Scrum Master orchestrates sprint reviews and product demos that showcase results transparently while encouraging dialogue rather than status reporting. These sessions allow stakeholders to see progress, validate direction, and contribute insights that guide future iterations. The Scrum Master ensures that these events stay focused on value, evidence, and collaboration rather than formality.

Practical techniques for stakeholder alignment include:

- Preparing concise summaries that connect sprint results to business objectives.
- Highlighting trade-offs and decisions made during the sprint to promote shared understanding.
- Capturing feedback systematically and translating it into backlog adjustments.

When stakeholders experience clarity and responsiveness, their confidence in Agile delivery deepens. Over time, this engagement transforms organizational behavior—from command-driven oversight to outcome-based partnership. The Scrum Master becomes a cultural connector, ensuring that collaboration extends beyond team boundaries.

Sustaining the Mental Model: Continuous Learning and Role Evolution

The Scrum Master role evolves with the maturity of the organization. At the team level, the focus is facilitation and flow; at the enterprise level, it expands into coaching leaders, improving systems, and influencing cultural change. This progression demands continuous learning and reflection.

Experienced Scrum Masters regularly assess their performance using metrics that capture both outcomes and relationships. Questions that drive reflection include:

- Are team decisions improving delivery predictability?
- Is the team adapting to change faster than before?
- Have I enabled psychological safety and accountability to grow together?

Reflecting on these indicators turns experience into actionable learning. The Scrum Master uses retrospectives, mentorship, and peer communities to gather feedback and refine practice.

Adopting new stances is another hallmark of growth. A Scrum Master who once focused on event facilitation learns to act as an organizational coach, systems thinker, or transformation leader. The ability to shift stances fluidly ensures relevance across evolving contexts. Whether leading a single squad or influencing enterprise governance, the guiding principles remain the same— empirical learning, transparency, and alignment around value.

Maintaining this mindset also requires resilience. As organizations scale Agile practices, conflicts emerge between traditional control mechanisms and adaptive leadership. The Scrum Master's role is to sustain constructive dialogue, proving through data and results that empowered teams outperform managed teams over time. This persistence gradually changes how organizations define accountability and success.

The Scrum Master's true mandate integrates leadership, systems thinking, measurable outcomes, and scaling influence. They cultivate disciplined autonomy, guide data-driven improvement, and connect team learning with business strategy. Each stance— servant, facilitator, coach, or change agent—serves a common purpose: enabling delivery systems that learn and adapt continuously.

For Scrum Masters, Agile Coaches, and Project Managers reflecting on their own roles, a few guiding questions remain useful:

- How am I enabling decisions that improve flow and learning across boundaries?

- Are our metrics serving the team or simply reporting to management?

- What behaviors am I modeling that reinforce adaptability and trust?

As Agile matures across enterprises, the Scrum Master becomes a strategic partner rather than a support role. Their work bridges the gap between iteration and impact, ensuring that Agile practices yield tangible business results. The next chapter explores this link further—how metrics, forecasting, and business outcomes validate the effectiveness of the Scrum Master's mandate within the larger organizational system.

Chapter 3 — Building High-Trust, High-Performance Teams

A Scrum Master's greatest influence lies in shaping the environment where collaboration, openness, and accountability can thrive. Teams that trust one another take initiative, learn from mistakes, and solve problems faster. This chapter explores the foundational element behind every high-performing Agile team—psychological safety. It examines how trust enables experimentation, supports constructive disagreement, and enhances adaptability. The sections ahead provide evidence-based insights and practical techniques for Scrum Masters to assess and strengthen safety within their teams, transforming ordinary groups into high-performing units that deliver consistent business value.

Psychological Safety — The Non-Negotiable Foundation

What Psychological Safety Is and Why It Drives Performance

Psychological safety is the shared belief that team members can express ideas, concerns, and mistakes without fear of embarrassment or retribution. It allows individuals to question assumptions, take intelligent risks, and learn collectively from failures. For Scrum teams, this safety directly influences agility—

the ability to respond to change depends on how freely people communicate, challenge, and adapt together[19].

Research shows that teams high in psychological safety demonstrate stronger problem-solving and innovation capability. McKinsey's organizational studies link these teams to improved productivity, faster decision-making, and stronger retention of talent. In the context of Agile, where learning and iteration are constant, safety forms the backbone of adaptability[20].

Scrum Masters serve as catalysts for this environment. Their facilitation style, feedback patterns, and transparency norms shape how team members interact. When a Scrum Master encourages openness during retrospectives, welcomes dissenting opinions in sprint reviews, and models humility by admitting personal errors, the message is clear—learning is valued over perfection.

Key conditions that emerge in psychologically safe Scrum teams include:

- **Candor:** Team members speak openly without filtering criticism.
- **Inclusion**: Every voice contributes to sprint discussions and planning.

[19]Gallo, Amy. 2023. "What Is Psychological Safety?" Harvard Business Review. February 15, 2023. https://hbr.org/2023/02/what-is-psychological-safety?

[20]Smet, Aaron De, Kim Rubenstein, Gunnar Schrah, and Mike Vierow. 2021. "Psychological Safety and the Critical Role of Leadership Development." McKinsey & Company. February 11, 2021. https://www.mckinsey.com/capabilities/people-and-organizational-performance/our-insights/psychological-safety-and-the-critical-role-of-leadership-development?.

- **Learning orientation:** Mistakes are treated as data for improvement.

- **Trust:** Feedback is shared with respect and constructive intent.

These traits do not develop overnight. They are cultivated through consistent, visible behavior from the Scrum Master and team leaders.

Common Misconceptions and How They Derail Teams

A frequent misunderstanding is that psychological safety equals comfort. In truth, a safe environment is often an uncomfortable one because it demands honesty, accountability, and vulnerability. A team that avoids disagreement to preserve harmony risks stagnation. When safety is reduced to politeness, difficult conversations disappear, and innovation suffers.

Scrum Masters must differentiate between comfort and trust. Comfort keeps conflict below the surface, while trust allows conflict to be addressed productively. Productive conflict clarifies ideas, strengthens decision-making, and reinforces shared ownership. Teams that view questioning as collaboration—rather than criticism—move faster because they align before acting.

To prevent misunderstanding, Scrum Masters can establish guardrails for productive challenge, such as:

- Clarifying that all feedback should target work, not individuals.

- Reinforcing that disagreement signals engagement, not defiance.

- Encouraging factual discussion backed by sprint data and metrics.

- Recognizing those who raise tough issues during reviews.

By setting expectations early, the Scrum Master makes open dialogue a normal part of the team's culture.

Diagnosing Your Team's Baseline

Assessing psychological safety requires attention to both visible and subtle signals. Scrum events—daily stand-ups, reviews, and retrospectives—reveal patterns that help diagnose the team's health.

Observable indicators include:

- Question frequency: Do team members ask clarifying questions during planning, or do they remain silent?

- Error acknowledgment: Are mistakes discussed openly, or handled privately?

- Feedback loops: Does the team adjust based on retrospective insights?

- Ownership: Are commitments distributed evenly, or centered on a few voices?

A Scrum Master can use quick pulse checks—short surveys or digital polls—to gauge sentiment. Questions such as "Do you feel comfortable raising a concern in this meeting?" or "Do you believe your ideas are valued?" can uncover early warning signs of disengagement.

Other methods include one-on-one coaching sessions where individuals can share concerns confidentially. Reviewing rework trends or repeated impediments also provides indirect data. If team members consistently redo work due to missed communication or unclear requirements, it may indicate hidden disagreement or fear of speaking up.

Tracking these signals over several sprints creates a baseline. Once patterns are identified, the Scrum Master can facilitate targeted actions to strengthen safety.

Practical Plays to Raise Safety

Building psychological safety is an ongoing process that combines leadership behaviors and structured team rituals. Scrum Masters can apply a series of micro-behaviors that steadily reinforce openness:

- Admit fallibility: Acknowledge mistakes to normalize imperfection.

- Invite dissent: Actively ask quieter members for input during meetings.

- Respond with curiosity: Replace defensive reactions with clarifying questions.

- Recognize contributions: Celebrate when someone identifies a risk or problem early.

These behaviors model humility and trust. Over time, they reshape how teams interpret feedback and manage risk.

Complementary team rituals further embed safety into Scrum practices:

- **"Red flag" check-ins**: Begin retrospectives by inviting members to mention concerns or uncertainties.

- **Decision logs**: Document key decisions and rationale to maintain transparency and accountability.

- **Blameless post-mortems**: After production issues, focus discussions on what was learned instead of who was at fault.

- **Speaking-order rotation**: Rotate facilitation roles in retrospectives or reviews to give each member equal influence.

These practices reinforce Scrum's inspect-and-adapt principle. By institutionalizing moments for honest reflection, the Scrum Master turns trust-building into a repeatable habit.

McKinsey research on team performance shows that organizations with leaders who demonstrate humility and inclusive decision-making outperform peers on innovation and retention metrics. When Scrum Masters embed these same habits, the impact compounds—teams feel safe to challenge assumptions, test ideas, and course-correct early[21].

Psychological safety is the foundation upon which every other team capability rests. Without it, continuous improvement becomes compliance rather than learning, and feedback loses meaning. The Scrum Master, as facilitator and cultural architect, carries the responsibility of making safety visible, measurable, and actionable across every sprint.

Team Dynamics and Conflict That Improves Work

Healthy vs. Destructive Conflict

Conflict is an unavoidable part of collaboration. When handled with structure and respect, it becomes a catalyst for innovation and

---

[21] Aaron De Smet et al. McKinsey & Company, 2021.

stronger alignment. Productive conflict focuses on ideas, data, and processes. Destructive conflict targets personalities and erodes trust. Teams that understand this difference learn faster and make better collective decisions[22].

There are three primary types of conflict that Scrum Masters should help teams recognize:

- **Task conflict:** Differences about what should be done or how to approach a problem. This type encourages diverse thinking when managed well.

- **Process conflict**: Disagreements about how work should flow—timelines, responsibilities, or methods. Excessive process conflict can lead to inefficiency if left unresolved.

- **Relationship conflict**: Tension stemming from personal differences, values, or communication styles. This is the most damaging form, as it distracts teams from shared objectives.

Healthy teams surface tasks   and process conflicts early. They focus on the content of disagreement instead of assigning blame. Scrum Masters can use sprint planning and reviews as safe forums for discussing misalignments about priorities or execution. When conflict occurs within these structured events, it becomes part of continuous improvement rather than disruption.

To maintain constructive tension, leaders should model calm inquiry. When voices rise or silence spreads, the Scrum Master's role is to reframe emotion into clarity. Questions such as "What outcome are we each trying to achieve?" or "Which assumption

---

[22]"4 Common Types of Team Conflict — and How to Resolve Them." 2024. Harvard Business Review. May 7, 2024. https://hbr.org/2024/05/4-common-types-of-team-conflict-and-how-to-resolve-them?

are we testing?" bring discussions back to purpose and data. Over time, this approach normalizes disagreement as a catalyst for improved work.

Conflict Resolution Toolbelt

Effective Scrum Masters utilize specific facilitation tools to maintain focused and balanced discussions. These techniques prevent escalation while allowing all perspectives to be heard. Each is rooted in evidence-based conflict resolution practices[23].

1. Surface interests before positions.

People often argue from their preferred positions rather than their underlying interests or needs. Before making a decision, the Scrum Master can guide the team in expressing what they truly seek. For instance, a developer pushing for automation may really want more stability, while a tester resisting it may be worried about lost visibility. By uncovering the shared goal, the team finds a solution that satisfies both perspectives.

2. Equal airtime protocol.

During intense debates, dominant voices can unintentionally silence others. Establishing a structured speaking order ensures inclusivity. The Scrum Master can set ground rules such as: each member shares one thought per round, no interruptions, and summarize the last point before adding a new one. This fosters balanced participation and slows discussions just enough for thoughtful listening.

---

[23]"5 Strategies for Conflict Resolution in the Workplace." 2023. Business Insights Blog. September 7, 2023. https://online.hbs.edu/blog/post/strategies-for-conflict-resolution-in-the-workplace?

3. Fact vs. interpretation board.

Teams often confuse data with opinion. Using a visible "two-column board" helps separate facts from assumptions. For example, "Sprint goal not met" belongs under facts; "The goal was unrealistic" belongs under interpretations. Once categorized, the team evaluates the facts first, then discusses interpretations as hypotheses to test. This simple method helps reduce defensiveness and clarifies the next steps.

4. Time-boxed optioning.

When debates drag, decision fatigue sets in. The Scrum Master can time-box discussions and conclude with shortlisting two or three actionable options. The team votes or experiments with one for the next sprint. This maintains continuous progress while allowing for flexibility to revisit the topic later.

5. Closure with ownership.

Every resolved issue should end with a clear owner and the next test. A documented follow-up, such as "Action: verify new deployment flow next sprint (Owner: Sam)," ensures accountability and learning. Re-examining these actions during retrospectives reinforces improvement loops.

Each of these techniques turns friction into a structured exploration process. When the team learns to apply them independently, the Scrum Master transitions from referee to mentor, empowering the group to self-correct.

Role of the Scrum Master in Hard Moments

Conflict is often a mirror of team maturity. Early-stage teams may rely heavily on the Scrum Master to mediate disagreements. As trust grows, the Scrum Master shifts to coaching the team in managing their own discussions. The goal is not to eliminate tension but to teach the team how to handle it productively[24].

Neutral facilitation is essential. The Scrum Master must avoid taking sides, even subtly. Neutrality allows all voices to feel valued and ensures discussions focus on outcomes, not personalities. The Scrum Master sets the tone by asking clarifying questions, rephrasing charged statements, and summarizing agreements as they emerge.

Reframing helps redirect emotional energy into constructive analysis. For example, transforming "This design will never work" into "What risks do we see with this design?" reduces defensiveness. Reframing encourages curiosity rather than confrontation.

Norm-setting gives teams behavioral boundaries for conflict. Norms may include assuming positive intent, challenging ideas respectfully, and using data to support claims. Revisiting these during retrospectives keeps them alive. When norms are visible and agreed upon, the team polices its own behavior, reducing dependency on the Scrum Master.

Conflict becomes most valuable during Scrum events that naturally involve differing perspectives:

- **Sprint Planning**: Aligning on what to deliver often sparks debate about priorities or capacity.
- **Sprint Review**: Stakeholders challenge outcomes, providing opportunities to improve transparency.

---

[24]"Psychological Safety: The Key to Team Success." 2023. Scrum.org. 2023. https://www.scrum.org/resources/blog/psychological-safety-key-team-success?

- **Retrospective**: The team discusses process and behavior improvements, making it the most critical event for resolving tension.

In these moments, the Scrum Master guides discussions toward experimentation. Instead of lengthy debates, the question becomes: *"What can we test in the next sprint to learn?"* This converts heat into progress and transforms disagreements into opportunities for adaptation.

The Scrum Master's maturity shows in how smoothly these conflicts are handled. A team that engages in direct yet respectful debate, commits to clear actions, and reflects on outcomes is a sign of strong facilitation and trust. Over time, these practices build a culture where conflict is seen as a signal of care—evidence that people are invested in achieving the best possible result.

Coaching Techniques that Scale Trust and Performance

Core Coaching Moves

Coaching in Agile settings is centered on observation, questioning, and guided experimentation. Scrum Masters who adopt a coaching mindset focus less on giving answers and more on enabling discovery. They observe team behaviors, listen for patterns, and prompt reflection that leads to action.

Effective coaching techniques include several core moves:

- **Ask powerful questions**: Open-ended questions like *"What would success look like by the next sprint?"* or *"What options have we not explored yet?"* provoke deeper thinking and ownership.

- **Focus on observable behavior**: Addressing specific actions rather than perceived intent prevents defensiveness. Instead of saying, *"You didn't collaborate,"* the coach might note, *"I noticed few comments on the shared board; what made collaboration difficult?"*

- **Use small experiments:** Encourage the team to test minor adjustments rather than sweeping changes. This keeps improvement manageable and evidence-driven.

- **Capture learning explicitly:** Each coaching conversation should end with a reflection or documented insight to sustain learning beyond the session[25].

These moves build autonomy and resilience. Over time, teams internalize reflective habits and become capable of diagnosing and resolving their own challenges. The Scrum Master then transitions from instructor to thinking partner—a sign that trust and maturity are taking root.

Coaching also reinforces psychological safety. When individuals are guided rather than corrected, they learn to view feedback as developmental rather than judgmental. This creates a safe structure for experimentation and collective learning.

Make Learning Visible

High-performing Scrum teams treat learning as work. They document insights, track outcomes, and adjust systems in full view of everyone involved. This visibility sustains accountability and connects daily actions to long-term improvement.

---

[25]Atlassian. 2025. "Retrospectives." Atlassian.2025. https://www.atlassian.com/team-playbook/plays/retrospective?

Scrum Masters can support this by maintaining three practical artifacts:

- **Improvement Backlog**: A visible list of actions identified during retrospectives, prioritized by impact and effort. Each item has a clear owner and expected outcome.

- **Retro Action Register**: A tracker showing completed, ongoing, and pending improvements. It prevents recurring issues from being forgotten and demonstrates continuous progress.

- **Evidence Board**: A visual map of experiments, showing the link between idea, action, and result—essentially, experiment → outcome → decision.

These tools make progress tangible. When learning outcomes are displayed alongside delivery metrics, the team sees that improvement work carries equal weight to product work. It also helps leaders appreciate the iterative nature of growth, reducing pressure for immediate results.

Google's research on high-performing teams highlights clarity and impact as critical dimensions alongside safety. Visibility provides both. When every team member can see why improvements were attempted and how they performed, trust increases. Transparency becomes proof of integrity—the team says what it will do and shows what it has done.

Scrum Masters can also amplify this visibility through brief updates in sprint reviews or internal newsletters. Sharing key learnings—such as "Reduced cycle time by refining acceptance criteria"—encourages other teams to replicate success. This practice turns isolated insights into collective knowledge across the organization.

Health Checks and Metrics Without Fear

Metrics can inform improvement or destroy morale, depending on how they are used. Scrum Masters must ensure data is used for dialogue, not evaluation. The purpose of measurement is to understand the system, not to rank individuals.

Practical health indicators to monitor include:

- **Cycle time:** How long it takes for work to move from start to finish.

- **Work in progress (WIP)**: How much the team is handling concurrently.

- **Impediment age:** How long blockers remain unresolved.

- **Engagement pulse:** Quick surveys on morale and workload balance.

- **Psychological safety check:** Periodic mini-surveys asking, "Do you feel safe voicing a concern?" or "Are your ideas valued?"

The Scrum Master reviews these data points to detect patterns and start conversations. For example, if cycle time rises while engagement drops, it may signal process friction or burnout. The coach then facilitates a discussion around system improvement, not blame.

Displaying metrics visually can help normalize transparency. Dashboards showing trends encourage curiosity and shared accountability. When people see their progress without judgment, they naturally align around solving problems. This is the foundation of trust—data as a tool for improvement, not inspection.

Building a rhythm around health checks also creates early warning signals. Instead of reacting to crises, Scrum Masters and teams proactively adjust behavior, capacity, or support structures. Over time, this discipline strengthens predictability and shared confidence in the team's ability to deliver.

Reset Quality Agreements

As teams grow, they often drift from the standards that once defined their success. Rework, unclear acceptance criteria, or inconsistent testing can erode trust within the group and with stakeholders. Re-establishing clear quality agreements revives pride in craftsmanship and accountability.

Scrum Masters can guide this reset through collaborative sessions that revisit the **DoD**, as discussed earlier. This exercise aligns everyone on what "complete" means for their context—covering documentation, testing, and deployment standards. When these expectations are explicit, confusion and handoff friction decline.

Reinforcing these agreements also strengthens the feedback loop between development and quality assurance. For instance, periodic reviews of the DoD in retrospectives allow the team to adjust for evolving technology or business needs. Aligning these expectations with service-level commitments restores stakeholder confidence and reduces rework.

Operating in Distributed and Cross-Team Settings

Remote and Hybrid Patterns That Preserve Trust

Remote and hybrid environments have changed how Scrum Masters build trust and cohesion. The physical distance between teammates can easily fragment collaboration if communication lacks rhythm or transparency. Scrum Masters must create deliberate structures that maintain connection and clarity.

A consistent communication rhythm provides stability. Daily stand-ups, sprint reviews, and retrospectives can remain effective when they combine asynchronous updates with live discussion. Written status summaries, recorded sprint reviews, and shared notes ensure every member stays informed regardless of time zone. This avoids unnecessary repetition while allowing teams to focus live sessions on problem-solving and decision-making.

Transparency replaces proximity in distributed work. Shared dashboards displaying sprint progress, impediments, and backlog changes help the team visualize commitments. A decision repository—a simple record of key discussions and outcomes—helps reduce confusion and maintains alignment visibility. It also helps new members integrate more quickly, as they can review past decisions and context independently.

Facilitation style matters even more in mixed time zones. The Scrum Master should alternate meeting times whenever possible and rotate the speaking order to prevent dominance by any one region. Inclusive facilitation tools, such as digital whiteboards or polls, ensure balanced participation. Small routines, such as "virtual coffee breaks" or "end-of-sprint gratitude rounds," humanize interactions and sustain rapport without overloading calendars.

Trust in remote teams is built through predictability and visibility. When commitments are clear, follow-up is consistent, and communication is transparent, distance becomes less relevant. These foundations allow distributed teams to operate with confidence and shared accountability.

Scrum of Scrums and Dependency Management

As organizations scale Agile across multiple teams, coordination becomes critical. Scrum Masters play a central role in ensuring that collaboration between teams preserves agility rather than creating bureaucracy. The Scrum of Scrums is a proven forum for managing dependencies and aligning release objectives across teams.

The purpose of the Scrum of Scrums is to share risks, interfaces, and upcoming release goals. It is not a status meeting. Each representative speaks briefly on three essential points:

- Progress toward the sprint or release goal.

- Impediments requiring support from another team.

- New dependencies or decisions affecting cross-team work.

A well-run Scrum of Scrums identifies integration risks early. For example, if two teams depend on the same API update, coordination happens before the bottleneck forms. The Scrum Master's job is to ensure that these meetings remain focused on forward-looking decisions, rather than backward-looking reporting.

Visualizing dependencies is key. Shared Kanban boards or integration maps that show cross-team handoffs provide everyone with visibility into workflow intersections. Marking items with dependency tags or color codes allows quick identification of blockers. When teams use this shared view, coordination moves from reactive to proactive.

The success of cross-team collaboration depends on discipline and brevity. Frequent short syncs are more valuable than long, infrequent ones. By keeping coordination lightweight and purpose-driven, Scrum Masters help multiple teams deliver cohesive outcomes while retaining their independence.

Tooling That Helps (and What to Avoid)

Technology enables distributed teams to collaborate effectively, but it can also introduce noise or over-monitoring if not used with intention. Scrum Masters should select tools that promote collaboration, transparency, and learning—while resisting those that encourage control or superficial measurement.

Useful categories of tools include:

- **Collaboration platforms**: Shared whiteboards, chat applications, and project boards that keep ideas visible and accessible.

- **Playbooks and templates:** Predefined canvases for sprint planning, retrospectives, and risk reviews that help standardize effective conversation structures.

- **Metrics dashboards:** Automated systems tracking flow metrics like cycle time, throughput, and impediment age to inform continuous improvement.

These tools are most effective when they serve communication, rather than compliance. The Scrum Master should regularly validate whether the team finds them helpful or distracting. Overlapping systems or dashboards with redundant metrics often lead to "tool fatigue," reducing engagement.

A common pitfall in scaled environments is metric theater—the use of dashboards to showcase numbers rather than insights. When teams report metrics to satisfy external audiences, data loses credibility. To prevent this, Scrum Masters emphasize context in every metric review. For instance, a drop in velocity may indicate necessary refactoring work, rather than inefficiency.

The discussion should focus on what was learned and how to improve predictability.

Tool-driven micromanagement also damages trust. Overly granular tracking of individual activity undermines autonomy and psychological safety. The Scrum Master must remind leadership that Agile metrics represent system performance, not personal evaluation. Healthy use of data is about learning, forecasting, and alignment.

When technology supports transparency, inclusivity, and learning, it becomes an ally. When used for surveillance or cosmetic reporting, it erodes the very trust Agile relies on. The Scrum Master's discernment determines which side the balance tips toward.

Real-World Patterns of Team Transformation

Project Aristotle as a North Star

Google's Project Aristotle provided one of the clearest insights into what makes teams consistently effective. Across diverse functions and skill levels, psychological safety emerged as the strongest predictor of sustained performance. High-performing teams shared a pattern of open voice, structured participation, and emotional awareness, which enabled members to surface concerns early and propose ideas without hesitation. These findings translate directly into the day-to-day environment of Agile teams, where discovery, refinement, and adaptation depend on frequent exchange of thought.

Scrum Masters influence these conditions through small but consistent behaviors: inviting dissent during planning, encouraging quieter members to speak first in refinement, and reinforcing norms that prioritize clarity over assumption. When these routines become habits, teams begin to experience the stability and openness that defined the most successful groups in Google's research.

Case Patterns You Can Replicate

Across industries, three recurring shifts have enabled teams to move from stress and inconsistency to healthier, more predictable delivery. Each shift centers on deliberate behaviors rather than large structural changes.

a) From blame to learning

Teams transform when failures become shared learning moments. Blameless reviews create a structured space to explore contributing factors without personalizing errors. Instead of asking, "Who missed this?" the discussion moves to questions such as:

- *What signals did we overlook?*
- *What was the earliest moment we could have spotted risk?*
- *What procedure or expectation needs clarification?*

This pattern reduces defensiveness and accelerates improvement. Over several sprints, teams start raising issues earlier because they trust that the environment supports honesty rather than penalty.

b) From hidden work to shared context

Many struggling teams operate with fragmented visibility. Tasks sit in private notes, blockers remain unspoken, and priorities shift without shared understanding. Visual flow practices address this.

- Boards that reflect real progress.

- Clear mapping of handoffs.

- Visible impediment lists with aging indicators.

When teams develop a shared view of their workflow, dependencies become easier to manage and coordination improves. This transparency also helps leadership see systemic constraints rather than attributing delays to individual performance.

c) From slow feedback to faster bets

Teams improve faster when review cycles tighten. Shorter sprint reviews, more frequent functional demos, and informal mid-sprint checks create earlier visibility into risks. Faster feedback reduces rework and refines assumptions before they solidify into commitments.

This pattern aligns with Agile principles: small experiments, frequent inspection, and timely adaptation. Scrum Masters strengthen this by ensuring every review connects delivered increments to intended value and by encouraging teams to test ideas with stakeholders rather than waiting for complete solutions.

Tying Trust to Outcomes Leaders Care About

Trust produces measurable outcomes, which is why executives respond strongly when Scrum Masters frame improvements in terms of business value. High psychological safety is correlated with higher engagement, which in turn influences productivity, learning speed, and reduced turnover. Teams with healthy dynamics onboard new members faster, adjust to priority changes more smoothly, and require less oversight, creating compound benefits over time.

Scrum Masters can report these outcomes in executive-friendly ways by:

- Highlighting predictability trends: variance reduction in sprint delivery and improvement in meeting sprint goals.

- Linking engagement signals to reduced rework and higher throughput.

- Presenting impediment-resolution speed as a proxy for team agility.

These measures turn trust from an abstract concept into a visible performance driver. When leaders see direct connections between team health and delivery confidence, they support the cultural and structural conditions that Scrum Masters advocate for.

Thus, high-trust, high-performance teams do not emerge spontaneously. They grow through intentional behaviors, clear norms, and consistent reinforcement from the Scrum Master. Psychological safety anchors this transformation, enabling teams to contribute openly and learn quickly. Healthy conflict and structured coaching practices guide teams toward deeper clarity, stronger collaboration, and faster problem-solving.

Distributed work and cross-team coordination introduce complexity, yet with deliberate communication patterns, transparent flow, and thoughtful facilitation, Scrum Masters can extend trust across distance and organizational layers. Real-world case patterns show that teams grow when learning replaces blame, when visibility replaces assumption, and when rapid feedback accelerates improvement.

By cultivating these conditions, Scrum Masters help organizations unlock engagement, predictability, and innovation—turning trust into a sustained competitive advantage.

Chapter 4 — Metrics That Matter to the Business

Agile ways of working generate a large volume of data, yet most organizations struggle to translate that information into insights that leaders trust. Teams often focus on points, burndowns, and sprint behaviors, while executives look for signals about value, risk, and delivery confidence. This gap creates friction and undermines belief in Agile as a management system.

The purpose of this chapter is to bridge that divide by reframing metrics as tools for business decision-making. When measured and communicated well, metrics help leaders understand whether value is growing, risks are visible, and teams can adapt at a sustainable pace.

From Team Metrics to Business Outcomes

Why Traditional Agile Reporting Frustrates Executives

Executives often encounter agile metrics that feel disconnected from the decisions they must make. Story points, burndown charts, and sprint velocity highlight how a team works internally, but they do not reveal what those efforts mean for revenue, competitive advantage, or customer satisfaction. Leaders want clarity on value trajectory, risk exposure, and the likelihood of delivering outcomes within strategic timelines. When team-level metrics fail to answer those questions, they appear incomplete or irrelevant, even if they accurately describe delivery activity[26].

Another recurring issue is metric noise. Different teams frequently define the same metric in different ways. One team may count throughput as all completed items, while another counts only customer-facing increments. Burndown charts vary depending on estimation approaches. This inconsistency creates confusion and forces executives to compare numbers that represent different realities. Without a common language, leaders cannot aggregate performance or assess portfolio-wide progress[27].

Vanity dashboards compound the problem. Dashboards filled with colorful charts often show activity rather than impact. They create a perception of transparency but fail to provide actionable interpretation. When stakeholders repeatedly encounter metrics that do not help them make better decisions, trust erodes. Leaders begin assuming Agile metrics are tactical rather than strategic. That perception reduces support for empirical planning and weakens the credibility of the Scrum Master and Product Owner roles.

The result is a persistent gap between teams and business decision-makers. Teams believe they are reporting clearly, and executives feel they lack the information required to steer strategy. This misalignment reinforces old behaviors—heavy upfront planning, rigid forecasting, and status reporting disconnected

---

[26]"Metrics for Agile Projects." 2025. Pmi.org. 2025. https://www.pmi.org/learning/library/agile-metrics-progress-tracking-status-6564?

[27]"Top 10 Agile Metrics for Executives." 2025. Allconsultingfirms.com. June 24, 2025. https://www.allconsultingfirms.com/blog/top-10-agile-metrics-for-executives/

from actual delivery conditions. A more deliberate approach to measurement is required to rebuild alignment and confidence.

Framing Metrics Around Business Questions

The most effective way to solve this disconnect is to begin with the questions executives need answered rather than the metrics teams are accustomed to using. When metrics are framed around strategic decisions, leaders focus on insights rather than data volume.

Four core business questions provide a strong foundation:

- **Are we delivering value today?**
  Leaders want signals that current releases improve product usage, satisfaction, or revenue.

- **How much potential value is still untapped?**
  They need visibility into unrealized opportunities and whether the backlog reflects meaningful upside.

- **How quickly can we respond to change?**
  Responsiveness influences competitive positioning and risk mitigation.

- **How sustainably can we innovate?**
  Sustainable pacing, quality trends, and team health reveal whether future delivery is at risk.

These questions align directly with the four key value areas of the **Evidence-Based Management (EBM)** framework: Current Value, Unrealized Value, Time to Market, and Ability to Innovate. Each value area provides a structured lens for connecting agile measures with business outcomes. EBM shifts the conversation away from internal activity and toward evidence that supports customer and organizational impact[28].

Once organizations adopt these business questions as anchors, they gain clarity about which metrics matter and which can be retired. This approach avoids clutter and creates a consistent reporting language across multiple teams or product lines. More importantly, it gives executives a coherent narrative: where value is growing, where value remains locked, how fast the system can adapt, and what might constrain future progress.

The Scrum Master As Metrics Translator

Scrum Masters play a central role in connecting team-level data to business understanding. Their responsibility is not to own all metrics but to help leaders interpret the signals that matter. This requires fluency in both agile practices and organizational goals.

A key part of this mandate is helping Product Owners map existing team metrics into the EBM value areas. For example, cycle time and throughput inform Time to Market; usage analytics illuminate Current Value; technical debt indicators relate to Ability to Innovate. By guiding this mapping process, the Scrum Master ensures metrics carry meaning for the broader organization[29].

Facilitating review workshops is another critical practice. In these sessions, leaders and teams examine current measures and group

---

[28]"Becoming Agile: Evidence Based Management." 2019. Scrum.org. 2019. https://www.scrum.org/resources/blog/becoming-agile-evidence-based-management.

[29]"How to Measure Value with Evidence-Based Management." 2021. Scrum.org. 2021. https://www.scrum.org/resources/how-measure-value-evidence-based-management.

them into value, flow, quality, and predictability dimensions. This structure simplifies reporting and encourages shared understanding. It also creates space to discuss what each metric reveals and which decisions it should inform.

Finally, Scrum Masters must guard against over-engineering. Many organizations accumulate dozens of metrics across dashboards, reports, and tooling. Large metric inventories reduce clarity and dilute focus. The goal is a small, stable set of measures aligned with business questions and consistently defined per product or value stream. A restrained metrics ecosystem supports better decision-making and strengthens trust in agile insights.

Choosing Metrics That Matter – Value, Flow, Quality, Predictability

Customer and Business Value Metrics

Value metrics serve as the foundation for business-aligned measurement because they quantify whether the product is improving customer outcomes and contributing to strategic goals.

Metrics such as Net Promoter Score, customer satisfaction, feature usage, retention rate, churn, and revenue per user provide direct insight into how users experience the product. These indicators help leaders understand whether current releases improve loyalty, reduce friction, or strengthen engagement. They also reflect whether the product is delivering on the promises made in the roadmap or portfolio plan.

Scrum Masters help create an environment where value is measured through evidence rather than assumptions. Their role includes guiding Product Owners to express backlog items as value hypotheses. Each backlog item should describe what outcome is expected, how it will be observed, and what behavioral change will signal success. This orientation frames features as bets that require validation. It reinforces the idea that backlog items generate value only when they influence customer behavior or contribute to measurable goals.

Scrum Masters also support the translation of value metrics into meaningful discussions during Sprint Reviews. Usage trends, customer feedback, and outcome data can be surfaced in lightweight visualizations. These insights help stakeholders understand whether delivered increments are moving key value indicators. They also encourage more informed investment decisions by showing leaders where opportunity remains untapped. This strengthens alignment between product strategy and delivery efforts.

Value metrics become even more effective when connected to the organization's wider economic view. Customer lifetime value, acquisition cost, or cost-to-serve can enhance the understanding of Current Value and Unrealized Value. By teaching teams how these measures relate to decision-making, Scrum Masters help improve the product group's analytical maturity. Over time, this builds confidence in incremental delivery as a mechanism for exploring and unlocking value.

Flow and Time-To-Market Metrics

Flow metrics provide visibility into how effectively work moves from concept to release. These measures highlight the operational conditions that shape the team's ability to respond to changing priorities. Lead time, cycle time, throughput, work in progress, and flow efficiency are among the most informative indicators.

They show where work slows, where queues form, and where context switching or unclear priorities create friction[30].

Lead time captures the duration from request to completion. It gives stakeholders an understanding of responsiveness. Cycle time focuses on active work and exposes delays in the development or validation process. Throughput tracks how many work items are completed within a defined period. Taken together, these metrics form a view of delivery capability that is grounded in real performance rather than estimates or forecasts.

Flow efficiency compares active time to waiting time. Low efficiency often signals bottlenecks, unclear ownership, or slow handoffs. This metric can motivate conversations about collaboration patterns, team boundaries, or tooling. Scrum Masters can use these trends to highlight areas where the workflow is constrained and invite stakeholders to participate in improvements[31].

Interpreting flow trends is essential. Rising lead time while throughput stays flat indicates that work is sitting idle longer. This pattern may reflect excessive work in progress, dependencies across teams, or increased review overhead. A sudden drop in cycle time may signal improved collaboration or better backlog refinement. These insights help stakeholders assess whether delivery conditions support stable, repeatable outcomes.

---

[30]Tsonev, Nikolay. n.d. "6 Agile Metrics to Boost Work Delivery and Efficiency."Kanban Software for Agile Project Management.https://businessmap.io/agile/project-management/agile-metrics.

[31]Tsubota, Sam. 2020. "Measuring the Flow of Value Using Flow Metrics."Atlassian Community. September 25, 2020. https://community.atlassian.com/forums/Jira-Align-articles/Measuring-the-Flow-of-Value-Using-Flow-Metrics/ba-p/1490534.

Scrum Masters play a key role in making flow metrics accessible. Their responsibility is to help teams visualize work, analyze trends, and understand how system-level issues influence performance. They also help portfolio leaders interpret flow data across multiple teams. This builds awareness of systemic constraints and encourages cross-functional alignment.

Quality and Reliability Indicators

Quality metrics reveal how well the product meets expectations. They signal whether the product behaves consistently, supports user needs, and remains stable across releases. Common indicators include escaped defects, defect density, mean time to recovery, deployment failure rates, and rework ratios. These measures provide early signals of risk that can influence cost, reputation, and customer trust[32].

Escaped defects show the quality of testing and validation practices. High counts can indicate incomplete user stories, unclear acceptance criteria, or limited exploratory testing. Mean time to recovery highlights operational resilience. Teams with shorter recovery cycles tend to have stronger engineering practices and clearer deployment pathways. Rework ratios reveal hidden waste that lengthens delivery cycles.

Quality indicators are deeply tied to the cost of delay. Teams that frequently encounter failures spend more time fixing issues rather than advancing new values   . This slows innovation and reduces predictability. When quality declines, leaders often respond by imposing more oversight or additional layers of review. A more

---

[32]Chick, Timothy A, Will Hayes, Suz Miller, and Eileen Wrubel. 2014. "Agile Metrics: Progress Monitoring of Agile Contractors." ResearchGate.unknown. 2014.
https://www.researchgate.net/publication/266049888_Agile_Metrics_Progress_Monitoring_of_Agile_Contractors

productive approach is to identify patterns and treat them as learning opportunities.

Scrum Masters help teams use these measures constructively. They create an environment where quality metrics trigger conversations about improvement rather than blame. They also reinforce the relationship between quality and sustainable pace. High rework rates or recurring production incidents signal that the team's operating system needs attention. Making these issues visible encourages investment in refactoring, better testing infrastructure, or a clearer definition of done.

Quality metrics also help executives understand long-term risk. Declining stability or slow recovery trends affect customer satisfaction and brand trust. By connecting these signals to business outcomes, Scrum Masters help ensure that quality remains a strategic concern, not just a technical one.

Predictability and stakeholder confidence

Predictability metrics indicate how consistently a team meets its commitments and how reliably it can forecast future delivery. Stakeholders rely on these metrics to assess whether plans are realistic and whether the organization can respond to emerging opportunities. Key indicators include throughput stability, sprint goal achievement, and forecast accuracy.

Throughput stability reflects how much variation exists across sprints. Lower variation suggests that the team has predictable working patterns and fewer disruptions. High variation suggests inconsistent flow, unclear prioritization, or frequent interruptions. Leaders interpret these patterns to understand delivery risk.

Sprint goal achievement shows whether the team can translate plans into outcomes. Consistently missing sprint goals signals deeper issues such as unclear backlog items, shifting priorities, or overcommitment. A strong trend of achievement builds trust in team capability and helps improve stakeholder confidence.

Forecast accuracy provides stakeholders with realistic expectations. It is more meaningful when framed using confidence intervals or range-based predictions rather than single dates. Leaders value clarity about uncertainty. They need to understand the likelihood of meeting target releases rather than simply hearing a commitment.

Scrum Masters ensure that commitments reflect empirical performance rather than optimism. They encourage teams to plan based on actual throughput and cycle time data. They help stakeholders understand which factors influence predictability and what actions can improve stability. By managing expectations transparently, they strengthen credibility across the organization.

Predictability metrics also guide investment decisions. When teams demonstrate stability, leaders can fund larger initiatives with confidence. When variation increases, leaders may shift focus to reducing risk before scaling delivery. Aligning predictability with strategic planning supports better allocation of resources.

Forecasting, Risk Visibility, and Delivery Confidence

Limits of Traditional Estimation and Point Forecasts

Traditional forecasting methods rely heavily on deterministic plans and single-date commitments. These approaches work poorly in environments with shifting priorities, evolving requirements, and interconnected dependencies.

Teams that depend on story-point projections or fixed Gantt timelines often underestimate the variability inherent in complex product work. This mismatch between actual delivery patterns and planned timelines creates avoidable risk. Leaders receive projections that appear certain but are based on assumptions rather than evidence.

Over-confident forecasting has long-term consequences. When dates slip, teams accumulate technical debt as they rush to meet commitments. Quality declines and defects increase. Stakeholder trust erodes as plans must be revised repeatedly. Teams waste cycles explaining deviations instead of using time to refine planning models. These patterns rarely reflect poor intent. They arise because the mechanism for forecasting was never designed for uncertainty.

Scrum Masters help teams step away from these rigid methods. They encourage planning grounded in empirical performance, not idealized scenarios. This shift helps stakeholders understand that uncertainty is a characteristic of the work, not a failure of the team. It also prepares the environment for better forecasting practices that improve predictability.

Probabilistic forecasting with agile data

Probabilistic forecasting offers a more realistic view of delivery timelines. Instead of predicting a single date, forecasts present a range with associated confidence levels. This method uses historical throughput and cycle time to estimate when a certain amount of work is likely to finish. Because it draws from actual performance data, it better reflects real delivery patterns and variation.

One useful technique is Monte Carlo simulation. The method runs thousands of iterations using past throughput or cycle time data to model possible futures. It generates a distribution of outcomes.

These results help teams understand the likelihood of completing a backlog by a particular date or delivering a certain volume within a fixed period.

The Scrum Master guides teams in selecting the right inputs. Stable throughput patterns create more reliable simulations. Highly variable throughput highlights the need for system improvements before forecasting can hold weight. Once the simulation results are ready, they can be presented as confidence-based predictions such as "the model suggests an 85 percent likelihood of completing this scope within this range." This framing reduces the pressure on teams to commit to a single deadline and helps leaders understand uncertainty more clearly[33].

Probabilistic forecasting also works well with incremental planning. Teams can re-run models after each sprint. This creates rolling forecasts that change as conditions evolve. These updates help stakeholders make more informed decisions about scope, staffing, or release strategy.

Making Risk Visible Early

Forecasting alone does not prevent failure. Teams also need early signals about emerging risks. Agile delivery provides several operational metrics that function as risk indicators. These signals reveal when the flow is deteriorating or when delivery conditions are becoming unstable.

A few patterns help surface risk quickly:

---

[33]Cloarec, Jean. 2024. "Agile Probabilistic Planning and Forecasting: A Monte-Carlo Proposition." Medium. November 6, 2024. https://medium.com/%40jean.cloarec.k/agile-probabilistic-planning-and-forecasting-a-monte-carlo-proposition-aacf49fc7538.

- Lead time spikes usually indicate rising complexity, capacity gaps, or new dependencies.

- Declining throughput paired with rising work in progress suggests over-commitment or blocked work.

- Flow efficiency dropping can signal longer wait times and overloaded review steps.

These signals can be built into dashboards that visualize risk across the sprint or product cycle. Useful elements include risk burndown charts, heat maps for high-exposure areas, and impediment age tracking. Impediment age is especially important. When blockers stay unresolved for long periods, systemic constraints emerge. These issues influence predictability far more than individual team performance.

Scrum Masters help teams interpret risks during ceremonies. In Sprint Reviews, risk data can clarify trade-offs and help stakeholders decide whether to adjust expectations. In Retrospectives, teams can explore root causes behind rising wait times or slow recovery from defects. These discussions help teams shift from reacting to risk toward anticipating it.

Building Delivery Confidence with Evidence

Delivery confidence grows when organizations rely on evidence rather than assumptions. Rolling forecasts provide the foundation for this approach. Each sprint adds new data, allowing teams to refine predictions based on real delivery patterns. Teams can adjust plans, highlight emerging constraints, and recalibrate expectations before issues escalate.

Scrum Masters help present these updates clearly. Executives often need three pieces of information: what changed, what the team learned, and what adjustments are being made. These short updates can be integrated into existing governance forums. This keeps leadership informed while reducing the need for extensive reporting cycles.

Confidence grows when teams communicate uncertainty transparently. When leaders understand the probability behind forecasts, trust increases. They are less likely to impose unrealistic commitments and more willing to support system improvements. This transparency also improves cross-team coordination. When upstream groups see a realistic picture of progress, they can plan dependencies more effectively.

Evidence-based forecasting also supports long-term decision-making. Leaders can identify where to invest to improve flow or reduce risk. They can decide whether to increase capacity or focus on quality improvements. These choices help build a system that delivers reliably.

Designing Dashboards That Empower Stakeholders

Principles of Effective Agile Dashboards

Dashboards support decision-making by presenting a clear story of how the product and delivery system are performing. Their purpose is to help leaders act with confidence, not to collect charts for display. A strong dashboard highlights patterns, signals risks early, and makes trade-offs visible.

Effective dashboards follow a few design principles. Clarity ensures that each chart answers one question. Minimalism reduces noise so that stakeholders focus on the trends that matter. Visual hierarchy guides the eye from top priorities to supporting data. Grouping related metrics together creates context, especially when value, flow, and quality indicators influence one another.

Dashboards lose value when they contain too many widgets or when teams use different definitions for the same metric. Inconsistent views create confusion for stakeholders. To avoid this, each audience should see only the measures that matter to their decisions. A small, stable set of metrics helps reduce complexity and improve adoption.

Different Views for Different Audiences

Different stakeholders need different levels of visibility. A single dashboard cannot serve all purposes. Instead, multiple layers help each group find the relevant level of detail.

Executive View

Executives need an outcome-focused view that highlights whether the organization is delivering value. Helpful indicators include:

- Current Value and customer sentiment
- Time to Market trends
- Risk posture and exposure
- Predictability at the portfolio or product level

These views help leaders decide where to invest and where to remove impediments.

Product Owner View

Product Owners need insight into how customers behave. Useful elements include:

- Feature usage and adoption
- Customer satisfaction
- Segment performance
- Outcomes from experiments

These indicators help evaluate whether backlog items delivered the intended impact and guide future prioritization.

Team View

Delivery teams need operational metrics that help them improve daily work. These views often feature:

- Flow indicators
- Quality signals
- Impediment trends
- Sprint goal tracking

These metrics help teams understand constraints and focus on improvement.

The Scrum Master ensures coherence across these layers. Executive, product, and team dashboards should tell the same story at different zoom levels. Aligning definitions and ensuring consistent interpretation prevents misunderstandings and supports better collaboration across functions.

Avoiding metric theater and misuse

Metric theater occurs when dashboards look polished but have no influence on decisions. It often appears when teams focus on aesthetics rather than usefulness. Another warning sign is when stakeholders passively review metrics without adjusting priorities or removing constraints. This pattern reduces trust in Agile measurement and wastes effort.

Misuse also arises when metrics are used to compare teams or evaluate individuals. These practices encourage gaming and undermine psychological safety. They distort the purpose of measurement, which is to understand the system and improve it.

Metrics should guide thoughtful decisions, not compliance or competition.

- A few safeguards help maintain integrity:
- Define a clear purpose for each metric.
- Hold regular "metric review" sessions to refine definitions and retire outdated measures.
- Discuss how each metric influences decisions and whether it remains helpful.
- Track how often metrics lead to action. A metric that never leads to change may no longer serve a purpose.

These practices create an environment where metrics support curiosity, aligned action, and system improvement rather than pressure or fear.

Putting It Into Practice – The Scrum Master as Business Partner

Co-creating a metrics strategy with leadership

The Scrum Master strengthens business alignment by helping leadership agree on a shared measurement approach. This begins with collaborative workshops that use the Evidence-Based Management key value areas as a foundation. These sessions help leaders shift focus from feature output to value creation, responsiveness, innovation capacity, and long-term sustainability. The Scrum Master facilitates discussions that explore which indicators reflect the health of the product and which decisions these indicators must support.

Once the value areas are understood, the Scrum Master works with Product Owners and leaders to define a small set of outcomes and flow measures for each product or value stream. This reduces noise and ensures that teams concentrate on the metrics most relevant to their strategy. The selection covers value, time to market, quality, and predictability, but the exact balance depends on product maturity and market conditions.

Clear governance completes the strategy. Leadership and Scrum Masters agree on how often metrics are reviewed, which forums host these conversations, and who acts on the findings. Quarterly value reviews and monthly risk reviews are common patterns. These rhythms ensure that insights travel beyond the team and influence portfolio decisions. Regular governance also helps leaders respond early to changes in delivery capability or customer behavior.

Embedding metrics in everyday Scrum events

Metrics create impact only when used during routine work. Refinement and planning sessions benefit from the inclusion of flow and predictability data. Teams can use cycle time and throughput patterns to set realistic Sprint goals. This helps avoid excessive commitments and positions the team to deliver consistently.

Daily Scrums are another place where lightweight metrics support clarity. Teams can review flow indicators such as work in progress, blocked items, or aging work. These signals guide quick adjustments to maintain healthy movement of work. The Scrum Master helps teams interpret this information in a way that supports improvement rather than pressure.

Retrospectives are strengthened by quality and value signals. Patterns in escaped defects, rework trends, or customer feedback can surface improvement opportunities. These insights encourage teams to explore root causes rather than addressing symptoms. They also help create visibility for investments in testing, automation, or better backlog preparation.

Sprint Reviews benefit from an outcome focus. Instead of listing completed work, teams discuss how recent increments influenced value or flow. Movement in key indicators helps stakeholders understand progress in context and encourages richer dialogue about strategy, risk, or next steps. The Scrum Master ensures that the conversation remains grounded in evidence rather than perception.

Evolving the metrics ecosystem over time

Metrics lose relevance if they remain static. The Scrum Master encourages periodic reviews to confirm alignment with strategy, customer needs, and product maturity. Early-stage products may need a stronger focus on learning and value discovery, while mature products may emphasize predictability and quality. This review helps avoid situations where teams chase metrics that no longer reflect business priorities.

New measures may be added as capabilities grow. For instance, teams experimenting with new technologies may adopt metrics that reflect innovation capacity or experiment throughput. Conversely, legacy metrics should be retired when they create unintended behaviors. Removing metrics that drive waste or gaming helps protect a healthy culture.

The Scrum Master acts as a custodian of evidence throughout this evolution. Their responsibility is to ensure that measurement supports transparency, learning, and empiricism. They help the organization stay focused on value rather than vanity measures. This stewardship encourages balanced decision-making and reinforces a culture of continuous improvement.

This chapter positioned metrics as a mechanism for aligning delivery with business outcomes. By grounding measurement in value, flow, quality, and predictability, Scrum Masters help teams and leaders make informed decisions. Forecasting becomes more realistic, risks become visible earlier, and dashboards become tools that promote clarity rather than confusion.

The Scrum Master's contribution extends beyond facilitating events. They shape how evidence is collected, interpreted, and discussed across the organization. Their influence helps connect day-to-day delivery with long-term strategy. This partnership creates the conditions for sustainable performance and prepares the ground for the next chapter, which explores how these insights strengthen forecasting, communication, and strategic alignment.

Chapter 5 – Scaling Scrum Without Losing Its Soul

Scaling becomes a necessity when a single Scrum Team cannot deliver the scope, speed, or breadth a product demands. As products grow in complexity and organizations expand across markets, the pressure to coordinate multiple teams increases. Yet expanding Scrum introduces new risks. Without thoughtful design and disciplined leadership, scaling can add unnecessary overhead, weaken agility, and overwhelm teams with layers of process.

This chapter examines why organizations scale, what challenges scaling frameworks attempt to solve, and which principles must remain intact to preserve the essence of Scrum.

Why Scale at All? When One Team Is Not Enough

The Real Drivers Behind Scaling

Organizations scale for several legitimate strategic reasons. Some products require several teams contributing to a shared codebase or feature set, especially when platforms span mobile, web, and embedded systems. Other organizations operate in regulated environments and require specialized teams that work in parallel. Global markets also introduce complexity through multiple regions, languages, or compliance requirements. These situations push companies toward multi-team coordination as a necessity rather than an option[34].

There are also less productive motives behind scaling. Some leaders pursue scaling to promote uniformity across departments even when the product does not require it. Others adopt a scaling framework because another company uses it, or because it appears to offer structure in times of uncertainty. These motives often overlook the unique needs of the product and the organization's capabilities. They create rigid structures that mirror other companies instead of addressing local constraints[35].

Scaling prematurely introduces measurable risks. Coordination overhead increases as teams navigate dependencies, review cycles, and approvals. Focus becomes diluted when many groups share ownership of the same product areas. Learning slows because teams have fewer opportunities to experiment and adapt before planning cycles lock in decisions. These risks compound when scaling is introduced before teams have mastered basic

---

[34]Beecham, Sarah, Tony Clear, Ramesh Lal, and John Noll. 2021. "Do Scaling Agile Frameworks Address Global Software Development Risks? An Empirical Study."*Journal of Systems and Software* 171 (1): 110823. https://doi.org/10.1016/j.jss.2020.110823.

[35]Tandon, Bhavna. 2024. "Scaling Agile Frameworks: How Different Are They from Each Other?" Valuex2.com - ValueX2 Is Designed to Be an One-Stop Shop for All Your Agile and Scrum Requirements. Our Industry Leading Agile and Scrum Trainers and Consultants Will Ensure Success of Your Agile Transformation Journey. Valuex2.com. July 21, 2024. https://www.valuex2.com/scaling-agile-frameworks-how-different-are-they-from-each-other/.

Scrum practices. Studies show that early scaling amplifies inefficiencies that already exist at the single-team level[36].

A useful way to evaluate the need for scaling is to examine product goals. If the work cannot be completed by one team within a reasonable timeframe, or if specialized skills must collaborate on a shared outcome, scaling may provide value. If the product remains within the capability of one team, investing in deeper mastery of Scrum often produces better results than adding more structure.

Core Challenges Scaling Frameworks Try to Solve

Scaling frameworks exist because certain challenges appear consistently when multiple teams work on one product. The first major challenge is dependency management. When several teams develop features that must integrate, delays or gaps in coordination disrupt progress, this also affects the shared Definition of Done, which becomes harder to maintain when teams work at different cadences. Nexus and other frameworks attempt to formalize integration activities so that increments remain cohesive across teams.

A second challenge is aligning product strategy across many contributors. When dozens of people share a backlog, clarity of priorities becomes critical. Multiple locations or time zones introduce further complexity, especially when customer insights and feedback cycles differ across regions. Scaling requires

---

[36]Ozkan, Necmettin, and AycaTarhan. 2020. "Evaluation of Scrum-Based Agile Scaling Models for Causes of Scalability Challenges," January. https://doi.org/10.5220/0009390403650373.

mechanisms to synchronize backlog refinement, elaborate product goals, and communicate changes efficiently.

A third challenge is protecting team autonomy. As organizations add coordination layers, teams can lose the freedom to self-manage. Managers may unintentionally impose centralized control to handle dependencies. This reduces creativity, weakens continuous improvement, and encourages feature-factory behavior. Research highlights that successful scaling depends on the ability of teams to maintain ownership of their commitments while cooperating with other teams on shared goals[37].

These challenges help explain why scaling frameworks exist. They aim to create structure where structure is necessary, while keeping teams flexible and empowered. The Scrum Master plays an important role in ensuring that frameworks address real constraints rather than becoming administrative overlays.

Principles That Must Survive Any Scaling Choice

Regardless of the framework chosen, certain principles must remain intact for scaling to succeed. The first is empiricism. Frequent inspection of integrated increments keeps teams aligned with reality. It also helps leaders understand whether scaling efforts are improving outcomes or adding unnecessary weight.

Self-management is another principle that cannot be compromised. Each team should continue to determine how best to achieve its goals. Without self-management, teams lose

---

[37]Verwijs, Christiaan , and Daniel Russo. 2024. "Do Agile Scaling Approaches Make a Difference? An Empirical Comparison of Team Effectiveness across Popular Scaling Approaches."*Empirical Software Engineering* 29 (4).https://doi.org/10.1007/s10664-024-10481-5.

engagement and creativity, and improvements become slow or superficial. Cross-functional capability also becomes more important as teams depend on each other to deliver integrated increments.

Simplicity is the final principle that protects organizations from over-engineering their scaling model. Scaling should amplify clarity, not create bureaucracy. Adding practices or roles that do not increase transparency, integration quality, or learning reduces agility. Successful organizations scale only what adds value. They avoid unnecessary layers and focus on practices that help teams work together effectively.

These principles shape the rest of the chapter. As we explore frameworks, orchestration, and anti-patterns, the central theme remains consistent: scaling must serve the product, the teams, and the customer. It must enhance agility, not dilute it.

SAFe, LeSS, Nexus – Patterns, Trade-offs, and Fit

Nexus – extending Scrum with minimal additions

Nexus provides a lightweight way to scale Scrum when multiple teams work on the same product. Its design focuses on three to nine Scrum Teams that share one Product Backlog. A Nexus Integration Team supports the work by ensuring that integration remains continuous and by helping teams surface dependencies early. The goal is to extend Scrum without adding unnecessary structure. It builds on familiar artifacts and events so teams can adapt without major disruption.

The strongest aspect of Nexus is its focus on integration. Multi-team development fails when increments cannot be combined, so the framework emphasizes clear transparency around dependencies, integration issues, and shared ownership of the Definition of Done. Nexus events also encourage frequent inspection of integrated work rather than isolated team output. This supports alignment and reduces the risk of discovering problems late in the cycle.

Nexus works best when teams already maintain disciplined engineering practices. Continuous integration pipelines, automated testing, and modular architecture allow Nexus teams to integrate frequently. When these practices are weak, the integration team may become overwhelmed. Another common challenge arises when product boundaries are unclear. If ownership overlaps or responsibilities are fragmented, teams struggle to manage the volume of dependencies that emerge in a Nexus environment.

Although Nexus adds minimal structure, it requires a high level of rigor. Teams must practice transparency, technical excellence, and shared accountability for product outcomes. Organizations that expect scaling to fix poor team practices often find Nexus demanding because it exposes problems quickly.

LeSS – scaling by descaling the organization

LeSS takes a very different approach. Instead of adding layers to coordinate many teams, it reduces organizational complexity. It promotes a single Product Owner, a unified product backlog, and as few roles and reporting layers as possible. This creates a broad product view and encourages teams to collaborate directly rather than routing decisions through intermediaries. The philosophy aims to simplify the structure so teams can focus on value delivery. The core idea is that adding more processes usually reduces agility. LeSS seeks to remove processes where it does not contribute to learning or customer value.

The strengths of LeSS lie in its product-centric view. With one Product Owner and one backlog, teams share a unified understanding of priorities and desired outcomes. This reduces the coordination noise that occurs when multiple product leaders assign conflicting goals. LeSS also supports strong team autonomy. Teams are encouraged to select their work from the shared backlog based on capability and capacity. This flexibility helps teams respond faster to new information and customer insights. Research indicates that simplified structures often correlate with faster decision-making and more effective continuous improvement cycles.

However, LeSS requires substantial organizational change. Middle management roles may need to shift toward coaching, enabling, or system design roles. Traditional hierarchies may need restructuring. Reporting lines and incentives often require realignment to support a product-focused model. These changes demand leadership commitment and cultural readiness. Organizations that attempt to adopt LeSS without addressing these structural shifts struggle to make the framework work effectively.

LeSS fits organizations that value simplicity, empowerment, and system thinking. It works best where leaders are prepared to redesign organizational structures to support team autonomy. When adopted without this willingness, the framework becomes difficult to sustain.

SAFe – integrating Agile with portfolio and program governance

SAFe offers a more structured model for large enterprises. It organizes work across several layers: team, program, large solution, and portfolio. These layers provide mechanisms for aligning strategy, budgeting, architecture, and execution. SAFe also encourages synchronized cadences through activities like

Program Increment planning, which brings many teams together to coordinate goals and dependencies. For enterprises dealing with complex regulatory environments, multiple value streams, or extensive architecture, these structures provide needed predictability and alignment.

A major strength of SAFe is its integration of portfolio governance with agile delivery. Leaders gain visibility into how investments connect to product outcomes. Architecture and engineering practices are also integrated through roles focused on system design and quality. Large organizations that operate across many divisions benefit from this explicit structure because it clarifies accountability and enables cross-department coordination[38].

SAFe's depth brings trade-offs. Its many roles, artifacts, and events can introduce weight if adopted mechanically. Organizations sometimes misinterpret SAFe as a process to enforce rather than a set of principles that guide strategy and coordination. When used this way, it creates centralized planning habits that reduce team autonomy and slow decision cycles. Field experience frequently shows that SAFe's value depends heavily on leadership maturity and adherence to lean thinking. Without this, teams feel governed rather than empowered[39].

SAFe is suitable for enterprises that require coordination across many layers and that need mechanisms to align strategy and

[38]Eigner, Christoph, and Günter Fahrnberger. 2025. "Challenges in Scaling Agile Frameworks and Ways to Address Them with Scaled Agile Framework (SAFe) and Scrum of Scrums (SoS)." *Communications in Computer and Information Science*, 453–70.https://doi.org/10.1007/978-3-031-94263-1_25.

[39]BhavnaTandon, "Scaling Agile Frameworks: How Different Are They from Each Other?" *ValueX2.com*, 2024.

execution. Its success depends on thoughtful implementation and ongoing simplification rather than strict rule-following.

What Comparative Studies and Field Experience Tell Us

Research comparing scaling frameworks consistently highlights one finding. The choice of framework matters less than the presence of strong local leadership, team autonomy, and consistent continuous improvement. Teams succeed when leaders remove impediments quickly, maintain clear product boundaries, and support integrated increments. Teams struggle when coordination relies on status reporting instead of active problem solving[40].

Across many organizations, several patterns correlate with successful scaling:

- Patterns of success across frameworks

- Clear product boundaries that reduce conflicting priorities

- Effective integration practices supported by strong automation

- Coordination forums that focus on risks and dependencies rather than reporting

- Lightweight structures that evolve as teams learn

- Continuous investment in engineering excellence and technical quality

These patterns appear across Nexus, LeSS, and SAFe implementations. The framework provides structure, but

---

[40]ChristiaanVerwijs and Daniel Russo, "Do Agile Scaling Approaches Make a Difference?" *Empirical Software Engineering*, 2024.

outcomes depend on culture, leadership, and disciplined execution. Studies of cross-team coordination in scaled environments emphasize that shared understanding of the product and integrated increments has greater impact than any specific ceremony or role[41].

For leaders choosing a framework, the most practical approach is to start with the smallest structure that addresses real constraints. Every framework offers value, but none is a substitute for strong team practices. Scaling works best when frameworks support clarity, integration, and adaptability rather than adding layers that do not contribute to outcomes.

The Scrum Master's Role in Cross-Team Orchestration

New Responsibilities in a Scaled Environment

Scaling expands the Scrum Master's field of view. When several teams contribute to one product, the coordination demands increase. The Scrum Master helps teams surface dependencies early and supports integration planning so increments combine cleanly at the end of each iteration. This requires visibility into technical interfaces, sequencing, and shared milestones. The role becomes a steward of the shared cadence that keeps teams aligned and reduces drift between schedules and priorities.

A critical responsibility is helping teams keep sight of a single product vision. Multiple teams often generate diverse interpretations of what matters. The Scrum Master collaborates

---

[41]"Agile Scaling Frameworks - Scrum and SAFe, LeSS, Nexus." 2021. Nearshore Software Development Company - IT Outsourcing Services. July 8, 2021. https://nearshore-it.eu/articles/agile-scaling-frameworks-scrum-and-safe-less-nexus/.

with Product Owners to reinforce common goals and to ensure that planning conversations reflect the same outcome orientation across teams. This alignment protects product coherence and guides teams toward consistent value delivery.

Scrum Masters also operate as part of a wider facilitation network. In many scaled environments, a community of Scrum Masters or team coaches forms a coordination layer. This group aligns facilitation approaches, shares systemic impediments, and standardizes useful practices. In frameworks such as SAFe, this appears as the Scrum of Scrum Masters, which helps maintain continuity across many delivery groups.

Orchestrating Dependencies Without Becoming a Project Manager

The Scrum Master increases transparency around cross-team dependencies through simple, visual methods. Integrated boards show work across teams and reveal interactions between components. Dependency maps display which teams rely on each other for inputs or integrations. Risk radiators make delays and blockers visible so they can be addressed before they escalate. These tools support coordination without converting the Scrum Master into a task controller[42].

Scrum of Scrums and similar forums support coordination on shared risks, interface agreements, and readiness for integration. These meetings encourage open discussion of potential issues and help teams synchronize architectural decisions. The Scrum Master facilitates these exchanges to support learning and shared responsibility. The forums remain focused on problem-solving

---

[42]"The Role of a Scrum Master in Managing Dependencies across Teams | Agile Seekers." 2025. Agileseekers.com. 2025. https://agileseekers.com/blog/the-role-of-scrum-masters-in-managing-dependencies-across-teams.

rather than status reporting, which enables teams to manage their commitments effectively.

Clear guardrails preserve the team-driven nature of Scrum. Product Owners continue to own backlog priorities. Teams maintain control over their plans and estimates. The Scrum Master promotes conversations that help teams take responsibility for resolving dependencies. This avoids centralizing authority in the Scrum Master position and ensures that ownership remains with those doing the work.

Maintaining Team Health and Agility At Scale

As structures expand, teams can lose their sense of autonomy. A rise in coordination meetings, increased reporting, and larger backlogs often reduces the space available for improvement work. Signs of strain include declining morale, limited impact from retrospectives, and patterns that suggest teams are becoming production lines rather than adaptive problem solvers. The Scrum Master pays attention to these signals and uses them to guide interventions.

Psychological safety can weaken in large settings where many stakeholders influence decisions. The Scrum Master reinforces healthy team norms by encouraging open dialogue, validating concerns, and supporting teams during conflict. When coordination obligations multiply, the Scrum Master helps teams protect time for reflection, experimentation, and quality enhancements. This ensures that scaling does not reduce the team's ability to learn.

Leadership support is essential. The Scrum Master coaches leaders to remove structural impediments such as bottlenecks in approvals, restrictive governance rules, or unclear ownership boundaries. These changes create space for teams to work more effectively. When leaders act on systemic issues, teams avoid the pressure to push harder within constraints that limit their performance.

Coordinating Across Time Zones and Locations

Distributed teams require orchestration practices that reduce friction. Asynchronous updates allow progress to be shared without requiring everyone to be online at the same time. Overlapping working hours support short periods of live collaboration. Recorded demos help teams stay aligned even when schedules differ. Shared online workspaces also help teams track decisions and maintain a common understanding of the work.

Tools contribute to transparency, but they must be used with care. Excessive notifications and multiple overlapping platforms can create noise that reduces focus. The Scrum Master works with teams to streamline tool use, clarify which platforms serve which purpose, and limit unnecessary alerts. This improves communication and reduces cognitive load in global teams.

Translating Team Level Metrics into Executive Language

Executives do not think in story points or burndown charts. They think in revenue protection, customer retention, delivery confidence, cost control, and strategic timing. When a Scrum Master talks about velocity or cycle time without translating those signals into real business meaning, leadership tunes out because nothing in that conversation connects to their responsibilities. The gap is not created because the metrics are wrong. The gap is created because the language does not bridge delivery work to business impact.

The starting point is to understand what executives want from metrics. They do not want granularity. They want predictability. They want clarity on whether an initiative is on track or drifting.

They want early warnings before a commitment is in trouble. They want confidence that the teams are working on the right outcomes. They want a clear sense of risk and the ability to make informed decisions without getting dragged into operational detail. A Scrum Master becomes a strategic partner when they frame team signals in a way that answers those leadership questions.

Velocity is a common example of a misunderstood Agile metric. Teams use it to understand their delivery pattern. Executives see it and ask what the number means for deadlines and scope decisions. A Scrum Master solves this gap by shifting the conversation from the number itself to what that number represents. When velocity is stable, it signals predictable delivery. When velocity fluctuates, it signals uncertainty that might affect a date or scope boundary. Instead of saying the team delivered twenty story points, the Scrum Master frames it as the team delivering at a consistent pace that supports a realistic forecast for the target date. The metric becomes a risk signal, not a performance scoreboard.

Cycle time is another metric that becomes powerful when translated well. Teams talk about how long a work item takes from start to finish. Executives care about how long it takes to turn a decision into a result. A Scrum Master can explain that shorter cycle times mean the organization can test ideas faster and reduce the financial exposure of long bets. Longer cycle times indicate delayed feedback, slower validation, and higher risk of late discovery. This shifts the conversation from team mechanics to business agility.

Lead time carries similar value when framed correctly. It measures the time between a request and its fulfillment. Executives interpret this as customer responsiveness and operational efficiency. When a Scrum Master explains that long lead times signal bottlenecks or overloaded teams, executives understand that the issue is not speed alone but the structural conditions that block flow. The metric now becomes an entry point for investing in team capacity, better prioritization, or workflow improvements.

Burndown charts are another place where translation matters. Delivery teams use them to see if they are completing work consistently. Executives want to know if an initiative is trending toward success or if a date is at risk. Instead of showing the chart and describing the slope, a Scrum Master can highlight the trend and explain whether the team is on track, slightly behind, or drifting. The chart becomes a visual confirmation of a business message rather than an artifact that requires interpretation.

Forecasting is where this translation becomes even more valuable. Team level metrics allow Scrum Masters to provide probability based forecasts instead of exact date commitments. Executives are already familiar with probability ranges through finance and risk management. A Scrum Master can say that based on historical velocity and cycle time patterns, there is a seventy percent likelihood the initiative will complete by the target date. This speaks directly to leadership comfort with risk informed decision making. The team metrics remain intact, but the message is delivered in the same language executives use in other strategic reviews.

Another area where translation matters is in explaining what metrics do not say. A Scrum Master needs to clarify that higher velocity does not mean higher productivity. It does not compare teams and it does not measure output quality. Executives appreciate honest framing that avoids false signals. When a Scrum Master explains what a metric does and does not indicate, they build trust with leadership. That trust leads to better decision environments and fewer pressure driven misinterpretations.

Executives also need metrics that reflect alignment with strategy. Team level data can be aggregated to show how much capacity is being spent on core value initiatives versus urgent interruptions or unplanned work. A Scrum Master can translate a flow distribution chart into business terms by highlighting how much effort is supporting strategic goals and how much is consumed by churn or reactive work. This gives leadership a clear view of where resources are actually going and whether the organization is working on the right things.

Risk visibility is another executive priority that benefits from thoughtful translation. Team metrics can reveal early signals of risk through rising cycle times, increasing work in progress, unpredictable sprint outcomes, and excessive context switching. When a Scrum Master presents these signals as trends that may affect an initiative, leaders receive early notice and can adjust scope, staffing, or priorities before an issue becomes a major setback. This positions the Scrum Master as a steward of organizational stability rather than a reporter of team problems.

The strongest translation happens when metrics are woven into a narrative rather than presented as disconnected charts. Executives respond better to structured explanations that follow a clear pattern. Current status, trend, risk, recommendation. A Scrum Master can explain that based on recent delivery patterns, the team remains on track. However, there is a rising trend in cycle time that may affect the next release window if not addressed. The recommendation is to reduce work in progress or clarify mandatory versus optional scope. The narrative connects the metric directly to decision making.

A good translation approach also avoids local optimization. Executives do not want to hear that a single team had a perfect sprint if the overall initiative is drifting. They want the end to end picture. A Scrum Master combines data from several teams to explain end to end flow stability. They highlight bottlenecks in shared services or upstream delays that affect downstream predictability. Leadership receives a cohesive view rather than isolated snapshots.

In large organizations, leadership dashboards often drown people in data without offering insight. A strong Scrum Master filters team level metrics to focus on the few signals that matter to executive decisions. These usually include predictability trend, delivery pace trend, flow stability, risk indicators, and scope versus capacity alignment. The goal is not to hide data but to elevate the data that holds real meaning for business outcomes.

Translation is not manipulation. It is clarity. It is the craft of connecting team activity to strategic goals. When a Scrum Master does this well, executives gain confidence that Agile delivery is not a black box. They see the connection between team behavior and business results. They make better decisions with fewer surprises. They trust the teams more. They trust the Scrum Master more. The entire organization benefits.

When team metrics are framed in this business focused language, executives stop asking for traditional project reports because they finally understand the value of Agile signals. The Scrum Master becomes a guide who gives leadership visibility they can use rather than detail they must decode. This is where the role moves from process facilitator to business partner, which is exactly what a modern organization needs.

Forecasting, Risk Visibility, and Delivery Confidence

Executives want to know one thing above all else. Can they trust the delivery plan? The question sounds simple, but it forces a Scrum Master to connect forecasting, risk visibility, and delivery confidence into a single narrative that leaders can rely on. Forecasting is not about predicting the future with precision. It is about giving leadership a realistic view of what is likely to happen based on real patterns in team behavior. Risk visibility is the practice of surfacing signals early enough for leaders to act. Delivery confidence is the outcome that appears when both are managed well.

Forecasting in Agile settings is probability based. Teams deliver in short cycles, which means they generate a steady stream of data that can be used to estimate future delivery. The mistake many organizations make is trying to turn this into a perfect date promise. A Scrum Master knows the real power comes from showing ranges and likelihoods. Executives are already used to probability based thinking because finance, market risk, and strategic modeling all use ranges. When a Scrum Master frames a forecast in that same familiar language, leaders can make decisions with far more clarity.

The starting point is understanding past performance. Teams that have stable velocity and consistent cycle time patterns create reliable signals. A Scrum Master uses those signals to create a forecast window. Instead of saying the project will be done in four sprints, the Scrum Master presents a range that reflects the delivery pattern. For example, the data might show a seventy percent probability of completing the target scope in four sprints and a ninety percent probability of completion within five sprints. This does not dilute the message. It strengthens it because leaders now see the risk profile, not just the best case scenario.

Forecasting also depends on the shape of the work. If the backlog is filled with small work items that move through the system at a steady rate, the forecast becomes more reliable. If the backlog contains large items with unclear boundaries, the forecast becomes fragile. A Scrum Master explains this to executives without drowning them in detail. They frame it as clarity risk. The more the work is sliced, the clearer the forecast becomes. The less refined the work is, the more the forecast behaves like a guess. Leaders understand clarity risk because it mirrors uncertainty in strategy decisions.

Risk visibility is the second half of this equation. Forecasts become useless when they are not paired with early warnings. Executives want to know when a commitment is sliding, not after it has already missed. Scrum Masters create visibility by watching the signals that shift before delivery collapses. These include rising cycle times, growing work in progress, repeated rollover work, unstable velocity trends, or increased interruptions. Each of these signals shows stress in the system before it becomes a missed deadline. When a Scrum Master brings these signals to leadership in plain business language, leaders gain the time needed to adjust scope or priorities.

The stronger Scrum Masters do not present these signals passively. They connect them to decisions. For example, they might say that the rise in cycle time indicates that flow is slowing and the initiative is at risk of slipping. They might recommend reducing work in progress or clarifying scope boundaries. They avoid leaving the executive with a problem and no guidance. This builds trust and positions the Scrum Master as an advisor rather than a reporter.

Delivery confidence emerges from the combination of forecast accuracy and risk transparency. Leaders do not need certainty. They need confidence that the team understands where they stand. A Scrum Master builds this confidence when they consistently give honest updates that match the reality of the work, even when the news is uncomfortable. Executives appreciate clarity far more than artificial optimism. A team that exposes risk early is seen as disciplined and trustworthy. A team that hides drift until the end is seen as unreliable, even if they work hard.

A concrete example makes this clearer. Imagine an organization preparing a customer facing release expected to launch in eight weeks. The team has a steady delivery pattern with an average of twenty points per sprint and low variance. The Scrum Master uses this data to create a probability forecast. They present a seventy percent likelihood of completing the planned work in eight weeks, with a ninety percent likelihood in nine weeks. Leadership understands the range and accepts it.

Two sprints later, the Scrum Master notices a rising trend in cycle time and an increase in partially completed stories. They investigate and discover that a dependency on the data team is creating delays. Instead of presenting this as a team struggle, they translate it into a risk message executives understand. They explain that the dependency is slowing flow and may affect the release window if left unresolved. They recommend either providing temporary support to the data team or reducing optional scope items. Leadership makes a decision quickly because the message is clear and framed in business language.

The outcome is simple. The risk is addressed early. The forecast remains stable. The release stays on track. Delivery confidence increases because the executives see the Scrum Master as someone who provides early clarity, not late surprises.

This example highlights the real power of a Scrum Master. They do not manipulate the numbers. They interpret them. They do not hide uncertainty. They expose it. They do not wait for risk to become a failure   . They address it early enough for leaders to act. This is what separates tactical Scrum Masters from strategic ones.

Another part of delivery confidence is teaching executives how to read patterns. A single dip in velocity does not matter. A downward trend does. A single sprint with spillover does not matter. Repeated spillover indicates misalignment between scope and capacity. A slight rise in cycle time may be noise. A sustained rise signals structural blockage. When a Scrum Master educates leadership on these patterns, they create a shared language that reduces confusion and frustration.

Forecasting also grows stronger when teams avoid over committing. High pressure environments often push teams to sign off on unrealistic delivery promises. This destroys credibility because every miss erodes trust. A Scrum Master protects delivery confidence by advocating for realistic commitments based on data, not optimism. Leaders appreciate this because it reduces strategic risk. No executive wants to base a key launch or investor message on a fantasy timeline. They want timelines rooted in empirical signals.

Scrum Masters also help executives understand the relationship between capacity and risk. If the team temporarily loses capacity due to vacations or on boarding, the forecast shifts. A Scrum Master explains this early. They present the new probability range and highlight the factors that changed. Leaders can then adjust scope or alter expectations before the date becomes unrealistic. Transparency becomes an asset rather than a weakness.

Delivery confidence also depends on showing progress in a way that matches executive expectations. Some leaders need trend based reporting. Others want simple traffic light views. Some want visual flow. A Scrum Master adapts the packaging to the leadership audience but keeps the message grounded in real data. The goal is not to impress with charts. The goal is to give leaders clarity in the format they absorb most easily.

Ultimately, forecasting, risk visibility, and delivery confidence are not separate activities. They form a continuous cycle. Forecasts guide expectations. Risk signals guide adjustment. Confidence emerges from disciplined clarity. A Scrum Master who masters this cycle becomes the person leadership trusts when making strategic decisions. They stop being seen as facilitators and start being seen as partners in execution. This is the real advancement of the role and the real value the business gains when forecasting and risk visibility are done well.

What Leadership Actually Wants to See in Scaled Settings

Leadership in scaled Agile environments is not looking for ceremony or compliance. They are looking for actionable insight and a clear line of sight into product outcomes. When organizations scale Scrum, the volume of data, meetings, and coordination increases dramatically. Without careful curation, executives can feel swamped with status reports yet remain blind to the actual health of the delivery engine. A strategic Scrum Master knows that what leaders want is visibility into progress, confidence in delivery, and early warning signals about risk. They want the story behind the numbers, not the numbers themselves. They want to make informed decisions, prioritize investments, and guide the business with minimal friction.

First, leadership wants clarity on outcomes rather than activities. In scaled settings, dozens of teams might be executing simultaneously, each producing output that appears meaningful in isolation but may not align with the overall product goal. Leaders are not interested in how many stories were completed or how many tasks were closed. They want to know if the product increment will achieve its intended impact for the customer and the business. For example, a multi-team initiative building a mobile app across iOS, Android, and web platforms will only be judged successful if users can experience the integrated features as expected. Leaders need assurance that cross-team dependencies are being managed, that increments are integrated, and that every team's output contributes to the overall value proposition.

Executives also want visibility into risk exposure. Scaled environments introduce complex interdependencies that can disrupt delivery if left unchecked. Leadership does not need a granular list of every risk, but they need to understand the critical points where delivery could falter. For instance, if the backend team is delayed and the API layer is a bottleneck for three other teams, leadership wants early awareness. They want the Scrum Master to frame this risk in business terms: what features might slip, how this impacts revenue or customer experience, and what mitigation strategies are in place. Presenting risk as a narrative tied to business impact is far more valuable than sharing technical charts or raw dependency matrices.

Another aspect executives focus on is delivery confidence. Leaders need to trust that the release plan is realistic and grounded in empirical data. They want confidence, not false certainty. A Scrum Master in a scaled setting demonstrates this by translating team metrics into executive language, showing trends, probabilities, and ranges rather than precise but fragile predictions. Confidence emerges when executives see that forecasts align with historical performance, capacity, and backlog refinement. It is reinforced when risk signals are surfaced early and mitigated proactively. Without this, leadership cannot make timely trade-offs or allocate resources effectively, and pressure cascades down to teams in ways that undermine agility.

Leadership also wants clear visibility into team autonomy and engagement. One of the most common failures in scaled environments is the erosion of self-management. Executives may notice signs such as consistent delays, misaligned priorities, or a lack of innovation from teams. These are symptoms of lost autonomy. They want to see that teams maintain ownership of commitments while still collaborating effectively. Scrum Masters communicate this by highlighting examples of decision making at the team level, demonstrating how teams resolved dependencies themselves, or showing how backlog priorities were adjusted through negotiation rather than top-down directives. Leaders want assurance that teams are empowered, learning, and capable of self-correction without constant intervention.

Another priority for leadership is integration health. In scaled environments, multiple teams produce interdependent components. Leaders do not need to see every integration test, but they do want to know that the product is consistently being assembled into a coherent whole. Executives care about whether the increments are integrated, tested, and deployable. Scrum Masters can provide simple, visual dashboards showing integration status, highlighting gaps, and pointing to any blockers that threaten the release. The emphasis is on insight into the state of the product as a single entity, not fragmented views of separate team outputs.

Transparency into strategic alignment is also high on the leadership agenda. Leaders want assurance that what teams are delivering matches business priorities. In scaled environments, misalignment is common, especially when multiple Product Owners or backlogs exist. Leadership needs clear reporting on whether features being developed address the right goals, generate expected value, and satisfy stakeholder expectations. Scrum Masters support this by tracking delivery against strategic objectives, summarizing priorities across teams, and surfacing conflicts that require leadership decision. This ensures that scaled delivery does not drift away from intended business outcomes.

Another critical element is predictability. While Agile emphasizes adaptability, leadership in large organizations still needs an understanding of timing, dependencies, and resource allocation. They want to see patterns of delivery, cadence stability, and known constraints so that planning and investment decisions can be made with confidence. A Scrum Master presents this without imposing artificial rigidity, using trends, probability ranges, and scenario analysis to show what can reasonably be delivered when. Predictability does not mean exact deadlines but means confidence in the expected direction and speed of delivery.

Leadership also values evidence of continuous improvement. They do not need details of each retrospective or improvement initiative. They want to see that teams are learning, adapting, and increasing their effectiveness over time. Metrics related to cycle time trends, defect density, and throughput improvements are useful when paired with stories of how teams applied insights to remove bottlenecks or improve quality. Demonstrating that the organization is systematically enhancing delivery capability reassures executives that scaling is not creating bureaucracy, but is instead enabling growth and efficiency.

Finally, leadership wants to see a structured but lightweight orchestration layer. They expect that the Scrum Master network, Scrum of Scrums, or cross-team facilitation forums exist and are effective, but they do not need operational detail. Leaders want evidence that these structures are serving the product and not creating overhead. They want to know that escalations are being surfaced appropriately, dependencies are managed, and teams remain focused on value delivery. A concise, clear update on how coordination supports outcomes is far more impactful than lists of meetings or artifacts.

A practical example illustrates this clearly. Consider an enterprise launching a new e-commerce platform requiring coordination across front-end, back-end, mobile, and operations teams in three countries. Leadership does not want a sprint-by-sprint account for each team. They want to know: are customers likely to experience a working platform on the target release date, where the highest risks are, are teams self-managing, is progress visible, and is work aligned with business priorities. The Scrum Master provides an executive dashboard showing overall completion versus forecast, risk heat maps highlighting integration dependencies, a summary of team autonomy practices, and a brief narrative on value alignment. Leaders can then make timely investment decisions, resource adjustments, or priority trade-offs without getting lost in operational detail. The result is transparency that is actionable, not overwhelming.

Dashboards That Help Rather Than Overwhelm

In scaled Scrum environments, dashboards can be a lifeline or a liability. Leaders, Product Owners, and Scrum Masters all need visibility into progress, risk, and performance. But raw data, overloaded charts, and excessive reporting can obscure insight instead of delivering it. The challenge is simple in concept but difficult in execution: how to provide meaningful visibility without creating cognitive overload or bureaucratic noise. Dashboards must inform, highlight trends, and enable decisions. They must reflect what matters for delivery, not just what is easy to measure.

The first principle is clarity of purpose. A dashboard must have a defined audience and specific intent. In scaled environments, there are multiple stakeholders with different needs: executives want high-level confidence and risk visibility, Product Owners need alignment on priorities, and Scrum Masters need insight into coordination and dependencies. Trying to create a single dashboard that serves everyone almost always fails. Instead, tailor dashboards to each audience. Executive dashboards should summarize delivery against strategic goals, highlight critical risks, and show trends in predictability and integration health. Operational dashboards for Scrum Masters can include dependency maps, sprint burndown, and team-level metrics translated into actionable insights. The key is avoiding a one-size-fits-all mentality that turns dashboards into noise.

Simplicity is the next guiding principle. Complexity does not equal insight. In scaled settings, dashboards often include dozens of charts, tables, and indicators, creating confusion. A well-designed dashboard prioritizes information that drives decision-making. For executives, this means a concise view of product readiness, feature delivery, and critical dependencies. Visual cues like traffic lights, heat maps, or simple trend lines convey complex information quickly. For instance, a red indicator on an integration risk map immediately draws attention to the teams or components at risk, prompting timely intervention. The goal is to reduce the mental effort needed to understand status while preserving depth for those who need it.

Effective dashboards highlight trends rather than single-point metrics. Metrics like velocity, cumulative flow, or defect counts are far more valuable when viewed over multiple sprints or increments. Leadership in scaled settings wants to see whether teams are improving, whether delivery predictability is stabilizing, and whether systemic bottlenecks are being addressed. A dashboard that updates daily but shows only the current sprint's velocity may appear busy but does not convey meaningful insight. Trend-based visualizations reveal patterns, support forecasting, and show where interventions are effective. For example, tracking the ratio of stories completed to stories committed across multiple teams over several sprints provides insight into predictability and team health, enabling leaders to take informed actions without micromanaging.

Contextualization is another critical principle. Raw numbers are meaningless without context. Teams and leadership must understand what a metric represents, why it matters, and what actions it suggests. A common mistake in scaled environments is dumping team-level metrics onto an executive dashboard without translation. Leaders do not care about story points completed; they care about feature readiness, risk exposure, and alignment with business goals. A Scrum Master can convert velocity or cycle time trends into delivery confidence percentages, projected completion ranges, or risk-adjusted forecasts. This allows leadership to see the implications for business outcomes rather than wrestling with technical detail.

Integration health should be central in any scaled Scrum dashboard. Multiple teams contribute to shared product increments, and integration issues often surface late, creating significant risk. Dashboards should surface integration status, highlight dependencies, and make gaps visible without overwhelming stakeholders. For example, a visual matrix showing which teams' outputs depend on others, combined with a simple indicator of integration success or blockers, provides immediate clarity. Leaders can see where interventions are needed, while Scrum Masters can focus on facilitating resolution rather than chasing status updates. The key is presenting a single source of truth for integration rather than fragmenting information across multiple systems or charts.

Dashboards should also support actionable decision-making rather than passive reporting. A table of raw metrics without interpretation is largely useless. Leaders need to know where to act, where to invest resources, and where to accept risk. Dashboards should highlight areas that require attention, summarize potential impacts, and, where appropriate, suggest mitigation strategies. For instance, a risk radar showing delayed dependencies can be accompanied by notes on likely impact on upcoming releases, allowing executives to adjust priorities, allocate additional resources, or approve contingency plans. Action-oriented dashboards transform data into insight and drive proactive management rather than reactive firefighting.

Automation and integration play a critical role in scaled settings. Data must be current and accurate, or trust in the dashboard erodes. Teams working across multiple tools and locations generate information in various formats, from version control systems to project tracking platforms. A well-integrated dashboard consolidates these inputs automatically, reducing manual effort and the risk of error. Automation ensures that dashboards remain timely and relevant, allowing leadership to focus on interpretation rather than collection. However, care must be taken to avoid over-automation. Dashboards should not become a passive display of every available metric; they must maintain relevance and context to avoid overwhelming stakeholders.

Another pitfall to avoid is "vanity metrics." Scaled environments often produce numerous measures, many of which do not influence delivery outcomes. For example, reporting total tasks completed across multiple teams might look impressive, but it provides no insight into whether features are integrated, working, or delivering value. Dashboards must focus on metrics that correlate with business impact, product readiness, and delivery confidence. Every data point should have a reason for inclusion, contributing to decision-making or situational awareness.

Dashboards should also facilitate transparency without micromanagement. Leadership should gain insight without dictating day-to-day team activities. For example, a dependency map or risk heat map shows where problems exist but does not assign blame or require executives to track individual tasks. Similarly, a trend line showing decreasing integration success over several sprints signals an issue that Scrum Masters and teams can address collaboratively. Dashboards empower leadership to make informed interventions while preserving team autonomy, which is crucial in scaled Agile environments.

Practical examples reinforce the value of thoughtful dashboards. You can consider an organization coordinating five teams across three continents, each responsible for different components of a cloud platform. Without a consolidated view, leadership struggles to understand whether delivery is on track. A well-designed executive dashboard aggregates team data into integration success rates, risk heat maps, predicted delivery windows, and feature readiness indicators. It summarizes trends over multiple sprints, shows where dependencies may delay releases, and highlights any alignment issues with strategic priorities. Leaders can then make decisions with confidence, and Scrum Masters can focus on removing impediments and facilitating cross-team coordination.

Finally, dashboards should evolve with the organization. Scaled environments are dynamic, and metrics that matter today may become irrelevant tomorrow. Regularly reviewing dashboard effectiveness, soliciting feedback from stakeholders, and adjusting metrics or visualizations ensures continued relevance. This also reinforces a culture of continuous improvement, where dashboards are tools to support learning and delivery rather than static artifacts. A flexible, evolving dashboard framework aligns with Agile principles while serving leadership needs effectively.

Avoiding "Scrum in Name Only" at Scale

How "Scrum in name only" emerges when scaling

As Scrum scales, organizations often preserve the language while quietly abandoning the intent. Events continue to exist, yet their purpose shifts. Sprint Reviews become reporting sessions. Daily Scrums turn into coordination briefings. Retrospectives lose influence as improvement actions are deferred or ignored. Teams deliver work, but integrated increments are missing, and progress is measured through plans rather than evidence.

Rigid role definitions also contribute to this pattern. Scrum Masters may be expected to enforce compliance instead of enabling learning. Product Owners may act as proxy managers rather than value stewards. Governance layers add approvals and checkpoints that reduce autonomy. Over time, Scrum terms remain visible, but decision-making reflects traditional command structures.

These symptoms usually originate from partial adoption of Scrum principles. Organizations adopt selected practices while keeping legacy management habits intact. Frameworks become checklists that teams follow mechanically. Empiricism weakens when leaders prioritize predictability through plans instead of learning through inspection. This disconnect creates a scaled system that appears Agile on the surface but behaves predictably and rigidly underneath.

Anti-patterns specific to scaled setups

Certain patterns appear frequently when scaling loses direction. One common example is the creation of a centralized coordination office where Scrum Masters are reassigned planning responsibilities. This shifts ownership away from teams and Product Owners and reintroduces dependency on central control.

Another pattern involves release trains or coordination layers that never inspect their own effectiveness. Planning cycles repeat without reflection. Risks persist across increments because integration problems remain unresolved. Without inspection, structures become permanent even when they fail to serve delivery goals.

Hardening or integration sprints also signal breakdown. When teams postpone integration to a later phase, defects accumulate, and learning slows. Continuous integration disappears, and quality becomes a late-stage concern rather than a built-in practice.

Stakeholder forums can also drift toward output tracking. Features are counted and deadlines reviewed, while value signals such as customer behavior, quality trends, or learning outcomes remain absent. These forums reinforce delivery pressure instead of supporting informed decision-making.

The cumulative impact of these anti-patterns is significant. Teams experience reduced engagement as autonomy declines. Stakeholders lose confidence when delivery issues surface late. Job satisfaction drops as roles become administrative rather than developmental. Research shows that environments dominated by rigid coordination structures struggle to sustain motivation and learning over time.

Guardrails to keep Scrum's soul when scaling

Scrum Masters play a critical role in protecting the principles that allow Scrum to function at scale. Certain elements must remain non-negotiable.

An integrated increment every sprint ensures that learning remains continuous. When teams produce releasable work together, problems surface early, and decisions rely on evidence rather than assumptions.

Empirical inspection of outcomes keeps attention on results rather than compliance. Reviews that examine customer impact, quality trends, and delivery signals reinforce transparency and learning.

Space for team-level retrospectives allows improvement to remain local and actionable. Even in large systems, teams need authority to adapt their working agreements and practices.

Clear product ownership preserves value focus. When accountability for value becomes diffused across layers, priorities fragment and teams lose direction.

Scrum Masters can also take practical actions to prevent drift:

- Start with a limited pilot when introducing scaling structures. Smaller Nexus or LeSS-style setups allow organizations to learn before committing broadly.

- Use anti-patterns as neutral discussion tools with leadership. Naming risks early helps leaders reconsider structures without assigning blame.

- Review scaling structures regularly. Ask whether the framework still serves the product or whether teams are serving the framework.

These actions help maintain alignment between principles and practice. They also create space for honest dialogue about what is helping and what is hindering delivery.

Avoiding "Scrum in name only" requires vigilance. Scaling magnifies existing behaviors, both healthy and unhealthy. When organizations preserve empiricism, autonomy, and value focus, Scrum remains resilient even as complexity increases. When those elements erode, structure replaces learning, and agility fades.

Chapter 6 – Executive Alignment and Stakeholder Influence

As Scrum expands beyond team boundaries, misalignment between strategy and delivery becomes a quiet risk. Teams may execute efficiently while leaders remain uncertain about direction, value, or trade-offs. This chapter focuses on the Scrum Master's role in closing that gap without slowing work or absorbing decision ownership. It explores how strategy can be translated into actionable goals, how alignment can be refreshed every Sprint, and how influence can be built without authority. The emphasis is on clarity, evidence, and relationships that allow strategy and delivery to evolve together rather than drift apart.

Bridging Strategy and Delivery Without Becoming a Bottleneck

Translating strategy into team-level clarity

Strategic intent often arrives in teams as broad statements about growth, efficiency, or market position. These statements carry importance but lack the specificity teams need to make daily trade-offs. The Scrum Master helps bridge this gap by guiding conversations that convert abstract direction into a shared Product Goal and a small number of Sprint Goals that connect work to outcomes the business recognizes.

This translation work begins by keeping language outcome-focused. Teams should understand how their work contributes to customer behavior, operational stability, or revenue protection rather than only feature completion. When Product Goals reflect these outcomes, Sprint Goals can be framed as measurable steps toward them, giving teams autonomy while preserving strategic coherence[43].

A practical way to support this translation is through a lightweight strategy-to-sprint mapping session. These sessions are short, focused, and designed to create shared understanding rather than documentation. A typical flow moves from intent to execution without adding layers of approval:

- Desired outcomes the business is pursuing
- Assumptions that must hold true for those outcomes to materialize
- Leading indicators that would signal progress or risk
- Backlog themes that express where effort should concentrate
- Sprint Goals that represent the next meaningful step

This approach allows teams to see how their backlog connects to strategy without requiring executives to micromanage delivery details. It also reduces last-minute priority shifts because assumptions and indicators are discussed early rather than discovered late[44].

[43] Schwaber, Ken, and Jeff Sutherland. 2020. "The 2020 Scrum Guide." Scrumguides.org. November 2020. https://scrumguides.org/scrum-guide.html.

[44] "Facilitation Tips for the Sprint Review." 2022. Scrum.org. 2022. https://www.scrum.org/resources/blog/facilitation-tips-sprint-review.

Building an alignment loop that repeats every Sprint

Alignment weakens when strategy discussions happen annually while delivery decisions occur weekly. Scrum offers a built-in rhythm to prevent this drift, but only if events are used for adaptation rather than reporting. The Scrum Master plays a key role in reinforcing Sprint Reviews as active checkpoints where product direction evolves based on evidence.

When Sprint Reviews are framed as approval gates, teams tend to optimize for presentation and certainty. When framed as inspection points, they invite discussion about what was learned, what changed in the environment, and what options are emerging. This shift allows executives and stakeholders to influence direction without rewriting plans outside the Scrum cadence.

To sustain this alignment, many organizations benefit from a simple stakeholder cadence layered on top of Scrum events. This cadence does not replace Sprint Reviews but adds predictability for strategic conversations:

- Monthly outcome reviews to discuss trends, risks, and emerging opportunities
- Quarterly direction checks to revisit Product Goals and major assumptions

Because these forums build on evidence already surfaced in Sprint Reviews, they avoid creating parallel governance structures. The Scrum Master supports this by ensuring discussions remain anchored in outcomes, learning, and trade-offs rather than task status.

Influencing without formal authority

In most organizations, Scrum Masters do not control budgets, staffing, or final priorities. Their impact depends on influence rather than authority. This influence is built through clarity, consistency, and trust, especially when executives hold decision rights that directly affect teams.

One effective influence practice is reducing ambiguity. When leaders clearly understand what decisions are needed, by when, and based on which evidence, they are more likely to engage constructively. The Scrum Master helps shape these decision moments by framing options, surfacing constraints, and clarifying consequences without advocating for a single outcome.

Another practice is influence through the community. Instead of resolving misalignment through escalation, Scrum Masters can convene cross-role working agreements that define how decisions are made and how conflicts are handled. These agreements often include shared definitions of readiness, escalation paths, and response times for executive input. Over time, they reduce friction by replacing ad hoc negotiation with predictable collaboration.

Research on influence without authority highlights that credibility grows when individuals consistently enable others to succeed rather than positioning themselves as intermediaries. For Scrum Masters, this means resisting the temptation to become a clearinghouse for decisions. Instead, they strengthen the system so Product Owners, teams, and leaders can interact directly within clear boundaries[45].

---

[45] Keller Johnson, Lauren. 2008. "Exerting Influence without Authority." Harvard Business Review. February 28, 2008. https://hbr.org/2008/02/exerting-influence-without-aut

When strategy and delivery are connected through shared goals, regular evidence-based checkpoints, and trust-driven influence, alignment becomes a continuous activity rather than a periodic correction. The Scrum Master's contribution lies in designing and protecting this flow, ensuring that clarity moves faster than confusion and that decisions are informed without becoming obstacles.

Stakeholder Architecture and Executive Alignment Mechanics

Map the stakeholder system, not just the stakeholder list

Many teams struggle with stakeholder management because they treat it as a list-building exercise rather than a system-design problem. A list of names does little to explain who influences decisions, who provides meaningful feedback, and who simply needs visibility. As products grow and organizations become more complex, this lack of clarity creates noise, delays, and contradictory signals that weaken both delivery and trust.

A more effective approach is to map stakeholders by how they interact with the product system. The Scrum Master can support the Product Owner by grouping stakeholders based on three practical dimensions: decision authority, impact area, and feedback value. This shifts the conversation from "who should attend meetings" to "how should different voices engage at different moments."

An engagement-focused stakeholder map typically distinguishes between:

- Stakeholders who make or ratify decisions that affect scope, funding, or strategic direction

- Stakeholders who provide insight through customer data, operational expertise, or regulatory knowledge
- Stakeholders who need visibility into progress and outcomes without influencing day-to-day priorities

Once these groups are clear, the team can explicitly agree on how each engages during Sprint Reviews, discovery cycles, and roadmap discussions. This clarity reduces unplanned interruptions and prevents feedback from being treated as a directive simply because of seniority.

A simple engagement map is often enough. It does not need tooling or formality. It only needs to answer three questions consistently: who needs to see progress, who is invited to give input, and who is accountable for decisions. When these answers are shared and visible, stakeholder behavior becomes more predictable and easier to manage.

Design executive alignment around business questions

Executive alignment weakens when discussions drift into delivery detail or status updates that add little decision value. Leaders rarely need to know how much work is complete. They need clarity on outcomes, risks, and the choices in front of them. The Scrum Master can shape alignment mechanics by designing conversations around business questions rather than activity reports.

Sprint Reviews provide a natural anchor for this alignment when they are structured around evidence and options. Instead of walking through completed items, teams can frame the review around a small set of questions executives already care about: what outcomes are emerging, what risks are visible, and what decisions may be required soon.

To support this, it helps to establish a shared vocabulary that allows leaders to participate meaningfully without pulling the team into status reporting. Terms such as value hypotheses, evidence signals, constraints, and decision points give structure to discussions and keep them focused on learning and direction rather than justification.

An executive-ready alignment agenda often includes:

- The Product Goal and whether recent evidence supports it
- Key signals from customer behavior, operations, or delivery flow
- Constraints that limit progress or introduce risk
- Near-term options that require guidance or trade-off decisions

This structure allows leaders to contribute where their input matters most while preserving team autonomy in execution. Over time, it builds confidence that engagement forums are worth attending because they influence direction rather than rehash progress.

Prevent stakeholder friction that damages team performance

Unmanaged stakeholder interaction creates friction that teams feel long before leaders notice. Common patterns include late-stage priority changes, fragmented requests from multiple executives, and informal side conversations that bypass the Product Backlog. These behaviors disrupt flow and erode confidence in the product system.

The Scrum Master plays a critical role in surfacing these patterns early and framing them as system issues rather than individual problems. When stakeholders understand how last-minute changes affect predictability, quality, and morale, they are more likely to adjust their behavior.

One effective intervention is facilitating explicit working agreements between the Product Owner, executives, and key stakeholders. These agreements clarify how work enters the backlog, when decisions are expected, and how escalations should occur. They also set boundaries around side channels by reinforcing the Product Backlog as the single source of truth for priorities.

Useful working agreement elements often include:

- Clear intake rules for new requests and urgent changes
- Decision timing expectations aligned with the Sprint boundaries
- Defined escalation paths for conflicts or strategic shifts
- Shared commitment to respect the Product Owner's accountability

By anchoring these agreements in Scrum accountabilities, the Scrum Master reinforces that alignment is a shared responsibility, not an enforcement role.

When stakeholder architecture is designed intentionally, executive alignment becomes easier to sustain. Leaders know when and how to engage, teams receive coherent direction, and decisions move through visible channels. The result is a system where influence flows through clarity and trust rather than interruption and escalation.

Sprint Reviews and Product Demos as Strategic Influence Platforms

Rebuild the Sprint Review into a working strategy forum

Sprint Reviews often lose their strategic value when they become predictable feature walkthroughs. When stakeholders attend as passive observers, the opportunity to influence direction, surface risk, and align on next steps is missed. Rebuilding the Review as a working strategy forum requires a deliberate shift in structure and intent.

The starting point is anchoring the conversation on progress toward the Product Goal. Instead of asking whether planned items were completed, the Review should examine whether recent work moved the product closer to its intended outcomes. This keeps attention on value, learning, and direction rather than task completion. Customer insights, early usage signals, and delivery constraints belong at the center of the discussion, alongside the increment itself.

Effective facilitation plays a major role here. The Scrum Master can guide participation by framing the Review around a small set of questions that invite contribution. Questions such as "What does this change in customer behavior suggest?" or "Which assumption feels weakest after seeing this increment?" help stakeholders engage as partners in discovery. This reduces the tendency to sit back and evaluate the team instead of collaborating with them.

Well-facilitated Reviews also make decision points explicit. Rather than hoping alignment emerges organically, the Scrum Master can signal when input is needed and what kind of input is useful. Over time, this builds a shared understanding that Sprint

Reviews are a place where strategy adapts based on evidence, not a ceremonial checkpoint.

Demo design that earns executive confidence

Executives tend to disengage from demos when they struggle to see how what they are viewing connects to outcomes they care about. A demo that earns confidence is concise, intentional, and framed around impact. It does not attempt to show everything. It shows what matters now.

Each demo segment should clearly link the increment to a user outcome or business signal. This might include early adoption patterns, operational readiness, or changes in support volume. Even when results are inconclusive, acknowledging what is still unknown builds credibility. Leaders respond better to transparency about learning than to polished presentations that avoid uncertainty[46].

A useful pattern is to include a brief evidence recap as part of the demo. This recap highlights what changed since the last Review, what was learned from those changes, and what decision or direction question follows. Keeping this recap short helps maintain momentum while ensuring that insight is not lost in the visuals.

This approach also helps prevent demos from drifting into technical explanation. Technical detail has its place, yet executive confidence grows when teams demonstrate control of outcomes, risks, and learning loops. The Scrum Master can support the team by rehearsing demo flow and ensuring that each segment answers a clear "why this matters" question.

---

[46] Atlassian. 2024. "Sprint Demo | Atlassian." Atlassian.com. Atlassian. July 18, 2024. https://www.atlassian.com/agile/project-management/sprint-demo?

Stakeholder participation standards

Sprint Reviews only function as influence platforms when stakeholder participation is intentional and constructive. Without shared expectations, Reviews can degrade into unstructured feedback sessions or live scope negotiations that disrupt focus and morale.

Defining participation standards helps protect both the team and the integrity of the Product Backlog. Stakeholders benefit from knowing what good participation looks like and how their input will be used. These standards do not need to be formal policies. They can be lightweight agreements reinforced through facilitation.

Helpful participation expectations often include:

- Arrive prepared, having reviewed prior context or metrics
- Focus feedback on outcomes, risks, and trade-offs rather than task-level changes
- Support decision-making by clarifying priorities and constraints
- Help remove impediments instead of introducing new scope mid-review

The Scrum Master plays a key role in reinforcing these behaviors during the Review. Timeboxing questions, using a visible parking lot for off-topic items, and redirecting new ideas into backlog refinement protect the flow of the session. This ensures that Reviews remain collaborative without becoming chaotic.

Protecting the team also means upholding Scrum accountabilities. Scope negotiation and prioritization belong with the Product Owner and the Product Backlog. When stakeholders attempt to bypass these mechanisms during a Review, the Scrum Master can gently redirect the conversation while preserving relationships. This keeps the event aligned with its purpose and prevents erosion of trust.

When Sprint Reviews and product demos are treated as strategic influence platforms, they become a powerful bridge between delivery and leadership. Executives gain confidence through evidence and clarity. Teams gain direction without micromanagement. The Scrum Master enables this exchange by shaping structure, facilitation, and participation so that strategy and learning evolve together.

Coaching Product Owners and Business Sponsors to Strengthen Partnership

Strong executive alignment depends less on formal structures and more on the quality of day-to-day partnerships. The Scrum Master plays a quiet but critical role in shaping how Product Owners and business sponsors interact with each other and with the teams. Coaching in this space focuses on clarity, decision discipline, and behaviors that sustain empiricism over time.

Coaching Product Owners on influence and clarity

Product Owners sit at the intersection of strategy, delivery, and stakeholder expectations. When they lack facilitation and influence skills, stakeholder conversations tend to generate noise rather than direction. The Scrum Master can help Product Owners shift these interactions toward outcomes and decisions.

One focus area is facilitation. Product Owners benefit from learning how to frame conversations so they converge on priorities and trade-offs. This includes setting a clear purpose for meetings, using structured questions, and closing discussions with explicit decisions or next steps. Over time, this reduces fragmented input and keeps backlog priorities coherent even as stakeholder interest grows.

Another coaching area is stakeholder management routines. Instead of reacting to requests as they appear, Product Owners can establish predictable touchpoints with key stakeholders. These routines clarify when input is expected, how feedback is incorporated, and what decisions can be made at each stage. When expectations are set early, escalations become less frequent and less disruptive.

The Scrum Master supports this growth by observing interactions, offering feedback, and occasionally co-facilitating high-stakes conversations until confidence builds.

Coaching business sponsors on how to support empiricism

Business sponsors often want to help, yet default to behaviors shaped by traditional governance models. Coaching here is about redirecting involvement toward actions that strengthen learning and reduce risk.

Sponsors add the most value when they enable faster decisions. This includes clarifying constraints, confirming priorities, and making funding choices that allow teams to test assumptions early. The Scrum Master can help sponsors see Sprint Reviews as opportunities to adjust direction based on evidence rather than as checkpoints for approval.

Another area of influence is flow enablement. Sponsors can actively support teams by removing organizational blockers, speeding up access to users, and approving small experiments without lengthy justification. These behaviors shorten feedback loops and reinforce empiricism as a leadership practice rather than a team-level technique.

Coaching sponsors often involve reframing success. Instead of asking whether plans were followed, sponsors learn to ask what was learned, what risk was reduced, and what decision is now clearer.

Operating agreements that keep alignment stable over time

Alignment degrades when decisions are implicit or when authority shifts depending on context. Lightweight operating agreements help prevent this drift by making expectations visible.

One effective practice is establishing simple decision agreements. These clarify who decides, by when, based on what evidence, and how trade-offs will be communicated. Such agreements reduce escalation and help stakeholders participate with confidence even when they lack formal authority.

Another stabilizing mechanism is a recurring alignment loop. This loop revisits outcomes, assumptions, and risks at regular intervals and confirms the focus for the next Sprint. When this cadence is maintained, executive engagement stays constructive and predictable rather than reactive.

The Scrum Master acts as a steward of these agreements, ensuring they remain practical and are adjusted as relationships and products evolve.

Executive alignment and stakeholder influence are not achieved through control or reporting layers. They emerge from clear goals, disciplined feedback loops, and partnerships grounded in trust and evidence. By coaching Product Owners and sponsors, shaping meaningful Reviews, and reinforcing operating agreements, the

Scrum Master helps organizations align strategy and delivery without slowing either. This work sustains focus, protects teams, and keeps decision-making anchored in learning rather than assumption.

Chapter 7 – Remote and Hybrid Facilitation Mastery

Remote and hybrid work have changed how Scrum Masters create clarity, trust, and momentum. Distance adds friction to communication, decision-making, and engagement, yet it also exposes weak facilitation quickly. This chapter focuses on practical facilitation approaches that help distributed teams think, decide, and improve together. The emphasis remains on human connection, disciplined structure, and outcomes that endure beyond the meeting's conclusion.

Remote-First Facilitation That Still Feels Human

Set the baseline: what "good facilitation" means when people are distributed

Remote facilitation succeeds when it produces the same outcomes expected in co-located settings: shared understanding, clear decisions, and next steps that actually move work forward. The Scrum Master's responsibility is to design interactions that make these outcomes visible, even when participants are separated by screens, locations, and time zones. Good facilitation in distributed environments is measured by what people leave with, not by how smoothly the meeting ran.

Several failure patterns appear repeatedly in remote teams. Silence with cameras off often hides confusion or disengagement. Parallel discussions in chat fragment attention and weaken alignment.

Meetings end without decisions, leading to follow-up debates in side channels. Over time, this "meeting residue" shows up as rework, delays, and frustration during delivery. Recognizing these patterns early allows the Scrum Master to adjust structure and expectations before they harden into norms.

Remote-first facilitation works best when each Scrum event is intentionally designed for visibility and focus. In the Daily Scrum, the emphasis stays on the Sprint Goal and immediate plan adjustments. Teams benefit from keeping work visible on a shared board and using brief updates tied to progress and obstacles. This prevents the session from drifting into status reporting for absent stakeholders and keeps ownership with the Developers.

Sprint Planning in distributed settings improves when preparation replaces prolonged negotiation. Capacity assumptions, known dependencies, and key risks are made visible before the live session. Shared visuals help teams explore options quickly and align on a realistic Sprint Goal. When planning time is used to make decisions instead of discovering unknowns, energy and clarity increase across time zones.

Remote-friendly design for core Scrum events

Sprint Reviews carry even more weight when teams are remote. These sessions work best as collaborative checkpoints rather than scripted walkthroughs. Showing evidence of outcomes, usage signals, and learning invites stakeholders into a real discussion. Clear decision prompts help participants focus on trade-offs and direction, reducing the tendency to observe passively or derail the conversation with late requests.

Retrospectives often determine whether remote teams continue improving or stagnate. Psychological safety grows when facilitation ensures equal participation and clear follow-through. Structured prompts, visible grouping of insights, and explicit action tracking help teams see that their input leads to change. Actions that are reviewed in the next Sprint reinforce trust and accountability, even when participants rarely overlap live.

Across all events, a few facilitation practices consistently help remote teams stay human and effective:

- Make decisions explicit and capture them visibly.
- Use structure to support participation, not to constrain it.
- End every session with clear owners and next steps.

When Scrum Masters focus on outcomes, visibility, and respectful engagement, remote facilitation becomes a strength rather than a limitation.

Tools as enablers, not the "process"

Tools should make teamwork easier, not louder. In remote and hybrid settings, teams often respond to coordination gaps by adding more apps, more boards, and more notifications. The result is scattered context and constant switching, which weakens focus and increases misunderstandings. A cleaner approach is to choose a small tool stack by purpose, then make it reliable.

Start with shared work visibility. A single board with clear workflow states and simple WIP signals helps everyone see progress and blockers without needing extra meetings. Pair that with decision capture. A lightweight decision log that records the owner, date, and rationale prevents repeated debates and stops decisions from living in private chats. Async updates also help when time zones do not overlap. Short written updates or quick recordings work best when they reference specific work items and call out blockers clearly. Finally, retro action tracking needs one stable home so improvement commitments remain visible and reviewed weekly, not forgotten after the session ends.

Guardrails protect teams from tool overload. Keep one source of truth for work and decisions, reduce notifications to what truly requires attention, and set norms that separate meeting topics from async updates, allowing people to stay aligned without staying online all day.

Engagement and Accountability Across Time Zones

Distributed teams lose momentum when facilitation assumes constant availability. Engagement across time zones improves when Scrum Masters design work around reality rather than ideal overlap. Research on remote collaboration shows that unclear expectations and unmanaged handoffs create silent delays that surface later as missed goals or rushed fixes.

Designing for overlap reality

The first practical move is mapping overlap windows. Teams benefit from explicitly identifying when collaboration is possible and protecting that time from low-value meetings. A clear meeting budget prevents calendar sprawl and preserves maker time for deep work. This clarity also reduces resentment when some members consistently attend meetings outside normal hours.

A stable cadence matters more than frequent contact. Predictable touchpoints for planning, review, and risk surfacing allow teams to prepare asynchronously and use live time for decisions. Async bridges between these events keep work flowing without requiring constant synchronization.

Helpful practices include:

- A shared overlap map visible to the whole team

- Fixed planning and review windows agreed at the team level
- Explicit use of async channels for updates and clarifications

Async rituals that keep work moving without micro-management

Async communication succeeds when it is structured and purpose-driven. Effective teams adopt a simple update format that focuses on progress, blockers, and next steps, always tied to the Sprint Goal and visible backlog items. This keeps accountability anchored in outcomes rather than activity.

Decision repositories reduce repeated debates. Capturing what was decided, why it mattered, what evidence supported it, and when it will be revisited prevents confusion across time zones. These records become a shared memory that supports continuity even when team members rarely overlap.

Lightweight escalation paths complete the system. Teams need clarity on how blockers surface, who responds, and what response time means in practice. This avoids stalled work without introducing control-heavy reporting.

Accountability mechanics that feel fair

Accountability improves when expectations are explicit and shared. Working agreements covering responsiveness, handoffs, and ownership reduce ambiguity in cross-time-zone workflows. These agreements remove the need for constant follow-ups because standards are already understood.

Clear definitions also matter. A well-understood Definition of Done, and a Definition of Ready where appropriate, reduces rework caused by misaligned assumptions. Agreement on how interrupts are handled protects flow and sets realistic expectations.

Participation design prevents engagement from collapsing onto a few voices. Rotating roles such as timekeeper, note owner, or decision scribe spreads responsibility and encourages broader contribution, especially in mixed-location meetings.

Case Patterns of Remote Scrum Success

Remote Scrum teams that perform well tend to rely on repeatable patterns rather than heroic facilitation. These patterns reduce coordination cost, improve learning speed, and help teams adapt without constant intervention.

What consistently works in remote and hybrid teams

Documentation acts as coordination. Writing down decisions, assumptions, and outcomes ensures distance does not create competing narratives. Teams that document lightly but consistently experience fewer misunderstandings and faster recovery from change.

Shorter feedback loops also matter. Frequent, smaller reviews lower delivery risk and surface issues earlier than infrequent large demos. This approach keeps stakeholders engaged and reduces late surprises.

Visible improvement reinforces trust. When retrospective actions are treated as real backlog items with owners and review dates, teams demonstrate that reflection leads to change rather than discussion alone.

Mini case library: patterns you can replicate

Pattern A: Async first, sync for decisions

Teams share context through pre-reads and async questions, then reserve meetings for evaluating options and making decisions. This reduces meeting length while improving decision quality[47].

Pattern B: Reviews that drive direction

Sprint Reviews focus on Product Goal progress, evidence, and trade-offs. Stakeholder questions feed refinement instead of triggering live scope negotiation, preserving momentum[48].

Pattern C: Retros that change behavior

Each Sprint includes one improvement experiment tracked through a simple loop: hypothesis, action, outcome, decision. This keeps learning concrete and measurable.

Measuring whether remote facilitation is improving performance

Evidence guides improvement. Useful signals include decision lead time, blocker age, cycle time stability, retro action completion rate, and the quality of stakeholder participation. These indicators show whether facilitation choices are reducing friction and strengthening accountability over time.

---

[47] "How to Embrace Asynchronous Communication for Remote Work." n.d. The GitLab Handbook. https://handbook.gitlab.com/handbook/company/culture/all-remote/asynchronous/.

[48] Okpara, Laura, Colin Werner, Adam Murray, and Daniela Damian. 2022. "A Case Study of Building Shared Understanding of Non-Functional Requirements in a Remote Software Organization." ArXiv.org. 2022. https://arxiv.org/abs/2205.09220.

A simple Remote Facilitation Scorecard can track these signals each Sprint and support continuous adjustment.

Remote and hybrid Scrum succeed through intentional design rather than constant presence. By respecting overlap limits, using structured async rituals, and applying proven patterns, Scrum Masters can sustain engagement and accountability across distance. The practices in this chapter help teams reduce silent delays, make decisions faster, and turn learning into action. When facilitation improves flow and trust, remote work becomes a reliable operating model rather than a compromise.

Chapter 8 – AI, Automation, and the Future of Agile Teams

AI and automation are beginning to shape how Agile teams plan, learn, and deliver. For Scrum Masters, this shift creates both opportunity and responsibility. Used intentionally, AI can improve clarity, accelerate learning cycles, and strengthen delivery confidence. Used poorly, it can weaken ownership and trust. This chapter focuses on how Scrum Masters can integrate AI into everyday Scrum work while preserving empiricism, team judgment, and ethical standards that keep Agile human-centered.

Where AI Changes the Day-to-Day Scrum Workflow

AI is already influencing the daily mechanics of Scrum. Its impact is most visible in refinement, estimation, and retrospectives, where teams handle large volumes of information and repeated decision-making. The value of AI in these areas comes from pattern recognition and preparation support. The risk appears when teams defer thinking to tools. The Scrum Master's responsibility is to shape how AI is used so it strengthens collaboration rather than replacing it.

Backlog Grooming and Refinement With AI Support

Backlog refinement is often constrained by fragmented information. Customer feedback arrives through multiple channels such as support tickets, surveys, sales conversations, and usage analytics. Teams review these inputs selectively, which makes prioritization vulnerable to bias and recency effects. AI changes this dynamic by clustering large data sets into themes that teams can inspect together.

AI tools can analyze qualitative feedback at scale and surface recurring patterns in user pain points, operational issues, or unmet needs. This allows Product Owners and teams to enter refinement with a clearer view of demand signals rather than isolated anecdotes. Human judgment remains essential. Teams still validate whether themes reflect meaningful opportunities or noise, but the starting point becomes more grounded[49].

AI also improves the quality of backlog items. It can assist in drafting acceptance criteria, identifying missing edge cases, and prompting dependency questions based on similar historical work. This reduces the likelihood of vague stories entering Sprint Planning. The benefit lies in coverage and speed, not authority. Scrum Masters should reinforce that AI output is a draft, reviewed and reshaped by the team before it becomes actionable.

Another important contribution is risk awareness during refinement. AI can flag uncertainty signals such as ambiguous language, repeated reopen cycles, unstable dependencies, or frequent clarification requests. These signals help teams identify work that carries hidden risk. Addressing uncertainty earlier reduces rework and improves Sprint predictability.

The facilitation challenge for Scrum Masters is ensuring refinement remains a collaborative learning activity. AI prepares the inputs, but conversations, trade-offs, and prioritization decisions remain human responsibilities. When refinement

---

[49] "Setup an AI-Powered Scrum Team (a Quick-Start Guide)." 2025. Scrum.org. 2025. https://www.scrum.org/resources/blog/setup-ai-powered-scrum-team-quick-start-guide.

becomes a review of AI output instead of a team discussion, value is lost.

Estimation and Forecasting Support

Estimation is an area where AI can improve discipline without promising accuracy. By analyzing delivery history, AI can summarize similar work, highlight hidden effort such as reviews or environment setup, and suggest options for slicing work into smaller increments. This helps teams build shared understanding faster.

AI support reduces time spent debating numbers and increases focus on assumptions, risks, and dependencies. When teams see that similar work previously required coordination or approval delays, they adjust expectations earlier. Estimation conversations become more concrete and less speculative.

AI also improves forecasting inputs by encouraging cleaner data. Consistent backlog descriptions, clearer workflow states, and reliable cycle-time signals make probabilistic forecasting easier to sustain. This supports forecasts expressed as ranges and confidence levels rather than fixed dates. Maintaining this discipline remains a human responsibility, guided by the Scrum Master.

A critical guardrail involves how estimates are used. AI suggestions can anchor teams toward false confidence if treated as commitments. Scrum Masters must reinforce that estimates exist to support planning and alignment, not performance evaluation. Trends and variability matter more than point predictions.

When facilitated well, AI shortens estimation sessions while improving their quality. Teams spend less time negotiating numbers and more time discussing delivery strategy and risk.

Retrospectives That Get Sharper, Faster

Retrospectives often lose effectiveness due to repetition and poor follow-through. Teams raise the same issues across Sprints while action items fade into the background. AI improves retrospectives by strengthening preparation and continuity.

AI can summarize recurring themes from past retrospectives, group-related feedback, and highlight which actions were completed or ignored. This provides historical context without manual effort. Teams enter retrospectives with clearer insight into patterns rather than starting from memory alone[50].

Action follow-through also improves with AI support. Drafting action items with suggested owners, success indicators, and review dates reduces ambiguity. Improvement work becomes visible across Sprints, reinforcing accountability without adding management overhead.

The greatest risk in AI-supported retrospectives involves psychological safety. If teams fear that notes or sentiment data may be used for evaluation, candor collapses. Scrum Masters must establish clear rules about what data is captured, where it is stored, and what never becomes evidence against individuals. Retrospective data exists to improve the system, not to judge people.

Effective facilitation keeps retrospectives human. AI organizes information and surfaces patterns, while the team interprets meaning and chooses actions. When this balance is maintained,

---

[50] "Retrospectives Reimagined: Inspiring, Data-Informed, Not Boring." 2025. Scrum.org. 2025. https://www.scrum.org/resources/blog/retrospectives-reimagined-inspiring-data-informed-not-boring.

retrospectives become shorter, sharper, and more impactful without sacrificing trust.

The Scrum Master Role in a Tech-Enabled Environment

AI changes the surface of Scrum work, but it does not change its intent. When summaries, drafts, and coordination tasks become automated, the Scrum Master's value shifts upward. The role becomes less about managing artifacts and more about shaping how work flows, how truth is maintained, and how learning stays real.

The Scrum Master as Workflow Designer, Not Tool Admin

In AI-enabled teams, the Scrum Master is not responsible for selecting tools or configuring prompts. Their responsibility is designing workflows that reduce friction without adding complexity. AI can automate meeting summaries, decision capture, and action tracking, yet these only help when embedded into simple, repeatable habits.

Effective Scrum Masters define where AI fits into the flow of work. For example, meeting summaries exist to shorten alignment time, not to replace participation. Decision logs exist to prevent re-litigation, not to centralize authority. Action tracking exists to sustain improvement, not to create surveillance.

To keep AI use lightweight, many teams benefit from standardizing usage through working agreements. These agreements clarify:

- Which tasks AI may assist with, such as drafting acceptance criteria or summarizing discussions

- Which areas are off-limits, such as performance feedback or personnel discussions
- How AI outputs are reviewed and approved before becoming part of the backlog or documentation

This approach prevents tool sprawl and keeps AI subordinate to team judgment rather than becoming a parallel process layer.

Protecting Empiricism and Truth in the System

AI-generated outputs often appear confident, which can mask errors or missing context. In Scrum, truth comes from inspection of real increments, stakeholder feedback, and observable outcomes. The Scrum Master safeguards this principle by framing AI as a hypothesis generator rather than a source of answers.

Teams need explicit expectations that AI drafts require validation. This validation happens through evidence, experiments, and customer interaction, not acceptance by default. Without this discipline, teams risk accelerating the production of plausible but incorrect assumptions.

Simple verification habits help preserve empiricism:

- Linking AI suggestions back to source data or historical work
- Making assumptions visible during refinement and planning
- Treating AI-supported insights as inputs to experiments, not conclusions

When Scrum Masters reinforce these habits, AI strengthens learning speed without eroding trust in evidence-based decision making.

Building Team Capability and Reducing AI Dependency

A common failure mode is silent skill erosion. Teams rely on AI to draft stories, summarize discussions, or structure retrospectives, then gradually lose their ability to do these activities well without assistance. Scrum Masters counter this by focusing on capability, not convenience.

Coaching shifts toward developing shared standards for AI-assisted artifacts. Teams agree on what "good" looks like for backlog items, retro outputs, and release notes, regardless of whether AI helped produce them. This often includes a definition of done for AI-assisted work that emphasizes clarity, testability, and alignment to goals.

Capability building also involves teaching teams how to evaluate AI output critically. This includes prompt discipline, checking for bias, and questioning missing perspectives. AI becomes a tool for thinking faster, not a shortcut around thinking.

Adoption should also be measured through outcomes rather than novelty. Useful signals include reduced rework, clearer backlog items, faster decision capture, and improved stakeholder understanding. When these outcomes do not improve, Scrum Masters pause adoption and adjust usage rather than pushing forward.

Ethical and Human-Centered Facilitation in an AI World

As AI becomes embedded in everyday Scrum work, ethical risks shift from abstract policy discussions to daily team behaviors. The Scrum Master plays a critical role in keeping trust, safety, and accountability intact while AI use expands.

Responsible Use Policies Teams Can Actually Follow

Teams need guidance that is clear enough to apply during real work. Overly complex governance slows delivery and gets ignored. Effective Scrum Masters help translate organizational policies into minimum viable rules that teams understand and remember.

These rules usually address three questions:

- What data is allowed, such as anonymized customer feedback or public documentation
- What data is prohibited, including personal data, confidential roadmaps, or internal evaluations
- How access and usage are reviewed and corrected over time

Ownership typically sits with leadership, but Scrum Masters reinforce these boundaries during refinement, reviews, and retrospectives. Governance becomes part of the workflow rather than an external audit layer.

Bias, Privacy, and Safety Risks Inside Everyday Agile Work

AI systems reflect the data they are trained on. In Agile contexts, this can amplify biases that already exist. Backlog prioritization may skew toward loud customers, short-term revenue signals, or easily measurable features while underrepresenting accessibility, technical risk, or long-term resilience.

Scrum Masters surface these risks during refinement by asking whose voice is missing and which outcomes are underrepresented. They also protect retrospectives from becoming surveillance tools. Sentiment analysis, note clustering, or pattern detection must never be used to evaluate individuals or rank teams.

Psychological safety depends on clear boundaries. Teams need confidence that reflection remains a learning space rather than a data source for judgment[51].

Human-Centered Facilitation Principles That Scale

Human accountability must remain explicit. AI may support decisions, yet humans own the consequences, trade-offs, and risks. Scrum Masters reinforce this by ensuring decisions are attributed to people and roles, not tools.

Risk management also becomes continuous. AI-related risks are identified, assessed, treated, and reviewed using the same iterative rhythms as product work. Sprint Reviews and Retrospectives become natural checkpoints for revisiting AI usage and its effects.

Many teams benefit from a simple AI Use Charter that includes:

- Purpose of AI usage
- Allowed use cases
- Banned data types
- Validation rules
- Storage expectations
- Review cadence

This charter evolves as teams learn, keeping AI aligned with Agile values rather than drifting into convenience-driven misuse.

AI will continue to change how Agile teams plan, learn, and deliver. The question is not whether Scrum Masters should use AI, but how intentionally they shape its role. By designing thoughtful workflows, protecting empiricism, and reinforcing ethical

---

[51] OECD. 2019. "The OECD Artificial Intelligence (AI) Principles." Oecd.ai. OECD. 2019. https://oecd.ai/en/ai-principles.

boundaries, Scrum Masters ensure AI strengthens clarity and learning without weakening trust or ownership. The future of Agile depends less on smarter tools and more on leaders who keep human judgment, accountability, and values at the center of increasingly automated systems.

Chapter 9 – Career Pathing: From Scrum Master to Strategic Leader

Career growth for Scrum Masters rarely comes from mastering more events or tools. It comes from expanding impact. This chapter focuses on the real shift that defines seniority in the role: moving from team-level facilitation to business-relevant leadership, while remaining grounded in Scrum accountabilities. It explores how Scrum Masters evolve their scope, identity, and influence so their work shapes outcomes leaders care about, not just team activity.

The Career Shift That Actually Matters

The most meaningful career progression for a Scrum Master is not a title change. It is a change in where their attention goes and how their contribution is measured. Early in the role, success is visible through smooth events and healthy teams. As the role matures, success becomes harder to see but far more valuable. It shows up in decision quality, delivery confidence, and an organization's ability to learn and adapt.

This shift requires understanding the distinct stages of impact and what actually changes at each stage.

Career Stages and What Changes at Each Stage

Stage A: Team-level excellence

At this stage, the Scrum Master's focus is on the team. The work centers on enabling effective Scrum events, supporting psychological safety, and removing impediments that slow progress. Strong Sprint Goals, clear backlogs, and honest retrospectives are the primary signals of success.

The value delivered here is reliability. Teams begin to trust their own plans and commitments. Stakeholders see steadier delivery and fewer surprises. While this stage is often treated as "entry-level," it forms the foundation for everything that follows. Without credibility at the team level, influence rarely scales.

Stage B: Multi-team influence

As organizations grow beyond a single Scrum Team, friction shifts from within the team to between teams. Dependencies, handoffs, and misaligned priorities become the dominant sources of delay. At this stage, the Scrum Master's work expands outward.

The focus moves to coordination patterns, shared working agreements, and cross-team risk visibility. The Scrum Master begins facilitating conversations across teams, often alongside other Scrum Masters, to surface integration risks early. Success here is measured by reduced surprises during integration, clearer ownership boundaries, and faster resolution of cross-team blockers.

Importantly, the Scrum Master does not become a central planner. The role remains facilitative. The value comes from helping teams see the system they are part of and adjust their behavior accordingly.

Stage C: System-level leadership

System-level leadership marks a clear shift from team mechanics to organizational outcomes. Here, the Scrum Master works across value streams rather than individual teams. Attention turns to flow, bottlenecks, and how decisions at the leadership level affect delivery capability.

Value stream thinking becomes essential. Metrics are no longer used to track team activity but to understand how work moves from idea to impact. The Scrum Master supports leaders in interpreting these signals and adjusting priorities, capacity, or policies.

Executive alignment loops begin to matter. Regular outcome reviews, risk discussions, and learning checkpoints replace ad hoc escalations. The Scrum Master's influence shows up in how leaders talk about work, not just how teams do it.

Stage D: Strategic leader

At the strategic level, the Scrum Master contributes to portfolio decisions, organizational design choices, and capability building. The work here is less about Scrum mechanics and more about preserving empiricism at scale.

Strategic leaders help organizations choose what not to do. They support trade-off decisions using evidence rather than opinion. They design structures that allow teams to learn quickly without excessive coordination overhead. Capability building becomes explicit, whether through communities of practice, leadership coaching, or evolving operating models.

The common thread across all stages is not authority, but clarity. Each stage requires a sharper understanding of where value is created and how decisions shape outcomes.

"Strategic Leadership" for Scrum Masters

Strategic leadership in the Scrum Master role does not mean writing strategy documents or setting corporate direction. It means shaping the conditions under which good strategic decisions are made.

One core behavior is improving decision quality. Scrum Masters do this by tightening feedback loops so leaders see evidence sooner. Instead of abstract progress updates, they help surface real signals such as customer response, delivery variability, and emerging risks. This keeps conversations grounded in reality rather than optimism.

Another behavior is protecting empiricism in leadership spaces. As organizations scale, it becomes tempting to replace learning with prediction. Scrum Masters act as quiet guardians against this drift. They ask what evidence supports a decision, what assumptions are being made, and how those assumptions will be tested in the next cycle.

Owning the operating system around delivery is also part of strategic leadership. This includes decision protocols, stakeholder architecture, and learning cadence. When these are unclear, teams absorb the cost through churn and rework. When they are explicit, teams can focus on solving problems rather than navigating politics.

The Leadership Identity Shift

The hardest part of career progression is not acquiring new skills. It is letting go of an old identity. Many Scrum Masters are rewarded early for being helpful, available, and deeply involved in team activity. Strategic impact requires stepping back from constant facilitation and stepping into design of the system itself.

The identity shifts from helping teams do Scrum to helping the organization benefit from Scrum. This does not reduce care for teams. It reframes it. Teams are supported by improving the environment they operate in, not by absorbing every problem on their behalf.

Trust becomes the primary currency. Strategic Scrum Masters build trust through evidence, clarity, and repeatable alignment mechanics. Metrics reviews focus on learning rather than performance. Outcome reviews clarify direction rather than justify past decisions. Risk reviews make uncertainty discussable before it becomes a crisis.

When this shift is made well, career progression becomes less about promotion and more about pull. Leaders seek out Scrum Masters who help them see clearly, decide responsibly, and adapt without drama. That is the point where the role becomes truly strategic, while still remaining faithful to Scrum's foundations.

Skill Stack, Mindset Shifts, and a Practical Development Plan words

Career progression for Scrum Masters rarely follows a linear checklist. It follows impact. The skills that differentiate senior practitioners are not additive extensions of facilitation basics. They represent a shift in how problems are framed, how influence is applied, and how learning is demonstrated across the system.

Power Skills That Differentiate Senior Scrum Masters

As Scrum Masters move into senior roles, facilitation expands beyond events into complex human dynamics. Conflict navigation becomes unavoidable. Senior practitioners learn to surface tension early, keep debate focused on work and outcomes, and prevent disagreement from becoming personal. This requires framing decisions clearly, naming trade-offs explicitly, and guiding groups toward closure rather than endless discussion.

Coaching capability also deepens. Instead of offering advice, senior Scrum Masters rely on behavior-based coaching. They observe patterns, reflect them back neutrally, and help teams experiment with new agreements. Protecting psychological safety becomes intentional work, especially when delivery pressure rises or leadership scrutiny increases.

Influence mechanics complete this skill set. Senior Scrum Masters design stakeholder contracts that clarify who decides, when input is needed, and how escalation works. They negotiate constraints rather than accept them as fixed. This allows teams to operate with fewer interruptions and a more predictable flow.

These skills share a common trait. They reduce organizational friction rather than absorbing it.

Business Fluency Without Losing Scrum Principles

Business fluency is often misunderstood as financial expertise. In practice, it is about understanding what leaders optimize for and how delivery signals connect to those concerns. Senior Scrum Masters learn to interpret value measures, risk exposure, and flow trade-offs in ways that resonate with decision makers.

This fluency shows up in conversations, not spreadsheets. Instead of reporting activity, Scrum Masters translate delivery data into confidence ranges, options, and constraints. They help leaders see how variability affects timelines, how bottlenecks limit throughput, and where small policy changes could unlock capacity.

Crucially, this translation does not dilute Scrum principles. Empiricism remains central. Evidence replaces assumptions. Feedback loops shorten. The Scrum Master's role is to ensure that business conversations stay grounded in observable reality rather than prediction theater (scrumguides.org).

"Evidence of Impact" Portfolio

As roles become more strategic, outcomes matter more than intentions. Senior Scrum Masters benefit from maintaining a lightweight evidence portfolio that demonstrates impact over time.

A practical format includes:

- Problem statement and context: What was not working and why it mattered.
- Intervention: What was changed, facilitated, or redesigned?
- Evidence used: Metrics, observations, and stakeholder feedback.
- Outcome: Shifts in delivery confidence, flow, quality, or decision speed.
- Learning: What was validated and what scaled next.

This portfolio aligns naturally with empiricism. It also provides a concrete way to communicate value during performance reviews, interviews, or promotion discussions without exaggeration or vague claims.

A 90-day development plan that compounds impact

Career growth accelerates when learning is structured. A focused 90-day plan keeps development grounded in real work.

- **Weeks 1–2:** Establish a baseline. Map key stakeholders, identify recurring friction points, and run a simple team health pulse.
- **Weeks 3–6:** Run two or three experiments. Examples include introducing a decision log, redesigning Sprint

Reviews around outcomes, or targeting a persistent flow blocker.

- **Weeks 7–10**: Demonstrate movement. Use evidence to show what changed and formalize working agreements that support the new behavior.
- **Weeks 11–13:** Scale learning. Share patterns through a community of practice, coach another Scrum Master, or improve a cross-team forum.

Promotion often follows when this cycle repeats consistently and visibly.

Certifications and Learning Paths That Match Real Career Moves

Certifications play a role in career progression, but their value lies in how well they support real capability building. Credentials work best as structure and signal, paired with demonstrated outcomes rather than treated as endpoints.

Scrum mastery progression

For Scrum Masters aiming to deepen their core practice, advanced Scrum mastery paths provide rigor around leadership, facilitation, and empiricism at scale. These programs focus less on mechanics and more on decision making, organizational impediments, and coaching leaders within the Scrum framework.

When chosen thoughtfully, these learning paths reinforce credibility. They also create shared language with other senior practitioners, which matters when influencing across teams or engaging executives.

Coaching track

Scrum Masters who gravitate toward coaching-heavy roles benefit from structured coaching education. These paths emphasize listening skills, powerful questioning, team dynamics, and change facilitation. The goal is not therapy. It is enabling groups to see themselves clearly and act deliberately.

Formal coaching education provides discipline. It helps Scrum Masters avoid rescuing behaviors and develop patience with emergence. This is particularly valuable when working with leadership teams or navigating deeply rooted organizational patterns.

Enterprise and scale track

For those moving into delivery leadership or enterprise roles, learning shifts toward operating models, cross-team facilitation, and large-scale coordination. These paths address portfolio alignment, dependency management, and governance patterns that either support or undermine agility.

The key is discernment. Senior Scrum Masters learn to apply just enough structure to solve real constraints without recreating command-and-control systems. Certifications in this space are most valuable when paired with hands-on experience in scaled environments.

Community-Recognized Credentials and Role Alignment

Industry-recognized credential ladders continue to influence hiring and promotion decisions. They offer signals of commitment and baseline knowledge. However, their impact increases when aligned with a clear role target.

165

- Coaching-oriented credentials support transitions into Agile Coach roles.
- Scale-focused learning aligns with Delivery Lead or enterprise facilitation paths.
- Value and product-oriented learning support movement toward product leadership.

Across all paths, continuing education matters more than accumulation. Senior Scrum Masters stay relevant by learning publicly, contributing to communities, and refining their practice in response to changing organizational needs.

Transition Paths and "What to Do Differently" in Each Role

When your title changes and you grow beyond the role of Scrum Master, your values, the people you influence, and the role you play in generating outcomes change completely.

That said, there are three natural transition paths most senior Scrum Masters find meaningful. These are Agile Coach, Delivery Lead/Flow Leader, and Product Leader.

Let's take a deeper look at these transitions as your impact grows:

Transition to Agile Coach

Moving into the role of an Agile Coach is usually the most natural next step for Scrum Masters who want to work systemically across teams and at multiple organizational layers.

As a Scrum Master, your arena is the team. You help them inspect, adapt, and remove impediments while keeping Scrum healthy. An Agile Coach keeps that foundation, but expands it:

- You regularly work with multiple teams (sometimes dozens), not just one.

- You coach Scrum Masters, Product Owners, and leaders, instead of just team members.
- In addition to team patterns, you also diagnose organizational patterns and help design interventions that stick.

Agile Coaches help people see structures instead of symptoms. They deepen the Agile mindset across roles and functions rather than just improving how Scrum events run.

So what's different in practice? Let's take a look:

- **Focus on system impediments:** Instead of zooming in on day-to-day blockers within a team, you start identifying patterns that repeat across teams, such as dependencies, feedback gaps, unclear leadership expectations, and misaligned incentives. Fixing those requires coaching leaders.
- **Become a coach to the coaches:** Agile Coaches spend a lot of time developing Scrum Masters, helping them internalize Agile principles, deepen their coaching presence, and manage complexity with confidence.
- **Run leadership workshops:** Agile Coaches also facilitate leadership and cross-functional workshops (for PI planning, value stream mapping, leadership alignment, etc.) that help leaders adopt an Agile mindset. This is a significant change in audience and impact from typical team retrospectives.[52]
- **Influence culture, not just process:** You help leaders reflect on behaviors that block agility, such as fixed budgets, over-reliance on commitments, or

---

[52] "How to Transition from Scrum Master to Agile Coach." Premieragile.com, 2025, premieragile.com/transition-scrum-master-to-agile-coach/. Accessed 9 Jan. 2026.

micromanagement. Changing culture is slower than fixing impediments, but it lasts longer.

Primary Outputs of an Agile Coach
- Enhanced capability building across teams and functions
- A coaching culture
- Reduced systemic blockers
- Leadership that understands how to support Agile practices
- Repeatable learning loops that scale beyond one team

To put it simply, Agile Coaches are facilitators who also serve as organizers of learning at scale.

Transition to Delivery Lead/Flow Leader

Another path that many senior Scrum Masters evolve into is a Delivery Lead or Flow Leader. These roles retain a connection to delivery outcomes while broadening their sphere of responsibility beyond team mechanics.

This role is especially common in organizations that don't distinguish clearly between Scrum Master and delivery leadership, or that explicitly use titles like Agile Delivery Lead or Delivery Manager.[53]

At this stage, your focus shifts from the performance of the Scrum to the predictability and sustainability of the entire system. That means:

- Flow governance over multiple streams of work
- Risk visibility at the program level

---

[53] Anderson, Jeff . "Agile Coach vs Scrum Master | Who Do We Need in Our Organization? - Agile by Design." Agilebydesign.com, 23 May 2024, www.agilebydesign.com/blog/agile-coach-vs-scrum-master-who-do-we-need-in-our-organization.

- Dependency orchestration across teams and stakeholders
- Bringing structure to forecasting and delivery cadence

You're no longer the person ensuring the Daily Scrum runs smoothly. Instead, you're ensuring several teams, or entire value streams, deliver together so that the business can count on them.

Here's what you do differently:

- **Manage flow and predictability over ceremonies:** Scrum Masters focus on helping teams improve their process. Delivery Leads focus on helping teams work together to deliver an integrated outcome, where delivery risk and expectations are visible and managed.
- **Form governance around delivery:** Instead of scheduling meetings and status updates, you help define decision cadences (e.g., weekly rolling forecasting, delivery confidence checkpoints) that keep information fresh without becoming overhead.
- **Clarify ownership and accountability:** You work with Product Owners, Delivery Managers, and program stakeholders to make sure:
    - Dependencies are visible early
    - Escalations trigger learning
    - Metrics reflect meaningful delivery outcomes
- **Build a stable metrics strategy:** Teams should own velocity and predictability. Delivery Leads own flow metrics that impact the business, e.g., throughput, lead time, risk exposure, and help teams use them to forecast with confidence. This is a different conversation from traditional "burndown charts."

Primary Outputs of a Delivery/Flow Leader
- Delivery confidence, even in uncertainty
- Shared visibility into risk and dependencies

- Cohesive cross-team execution rhythms
- Predictable outcomes rather than ad-hoc delivery
- A governance layer that supports teams without shattering autonomy

This path suits Scrum Masters who enjoy structuring complexity across teams.

Transition to Product Leader (or Product Operations)

Some Scrum Masters find their interests pull them toward the *"why"* rather than the *"how"* of product delivery. That naturally leads toward product leadership roles where shaping value becomes the primary focus.

It is different from becoming a traditional Product Owner. In this case, you lean toward product strategy, outcome measurement, and continuous learning.

When you make this transition, the most significant change is that you swap *ensuring good Scrum artifacts* for *ensuring meaningful product outcomes*.

Here's what you do differently:

- **Lead discovery:** Product leadership teams prioritize understanding user needs, forming hypotheses, and validating product assumptions, mostly with rapid experimentation and outcome-oriented feedback loops.
- **Operationalize outcome reviews:** Instead of attending Sprint Reviews to improve team flow, you design outcome review practices that help stakeholders decide:
  o Are features delivering value?
  o What do we learn with each release?
  o What do we change next?

- **Translate metrics into decisions:** Teams measure velocity and throughput. Product leaders measure customer impact, retention, and hypothesis validation— and use those metrics to guide investment decisions.
- **Reframe stakeholder conversations:** You stop talking about outputs and start talking about options, risks, and validated learning. The product backlog becomes a tool for experimenting toward value.

Primary Outputs of Product Leadership Roles
- Coherent product strategy that aligns with business goals
- A cadence of validated learning through experiments
- Clear linkage between delivery activity and business outcomes
- Stakeholder routines that sharpen decisions rather than justify work

This role is ideal for Scrum Masters who have always leaned into strategy, value definition, and business outcomes, and want a seat at the table where those decisions are made.

Building Influence Beyond the Team

No matter which path you pursue, a common set of practices strengthens your influence beyond individual teams. These are the building blocks that help Scrum Masters become architects of agreements.

To form a repeatable influence loop, you should:

- **Earn trust through evidence**. People are naturally skeptical of change. That's why evidence is important. It's a narrative built around what the data actually means, e.g., flow health, cycle time trends, decision lift, and outcomes achieved.

- **Convert friction into working agreements**. Whenever you see recurring tension, whether between teams, stakeholders, or leadership, breadcrumb a working agreement:
  - What's the tension?
  - What behavior or rule will reduce it?
  - How will we measure if it's actually helping?

  This pattern turns abstract friction into explicit agreements that teams can inspect and adapt.
- **Institutionalize what works.** Great practices shouldn't live only in retrospectives. When something repeatedly improves outcomes, be it a decision cadence, a risk checkpoint, or a cross-team sync, bake it into formal routines:
  - Communities of practice
  - Leadership learning loops
  - Standard decision frameworks

  Institutionalizing successful practices is how local influence becomes organizational muscle.

Influence in Scaled Contexts

In scaled environments (like SAFe, LeSS, or Nexus), streamlining with servant leadership expectations means you do less telling and more holding space:

You help leaders think in terms of value streams.

- You coach outcomes at the intersection of teams, customers, and corporate objectives.
- You protect empiricism by resisting the lure of prediction over experimentation.

Influence at this level is subtle. It helps others see patterns and options they couldn't see before.

Chapter 10 – Common Pitfalls and How to Overcome Them

Being a Scrum Master isn't always smooth sailing. Even with the best intentions and solid training, there are traps that catch many practitioners (and entire organizations) off guard. Pitfalls like burnout, surface-level Agile adoption, resistance to change, and misjudging when to step in or step back can slow teams, erode trust, and dim the impact of your work.

That's why it is important to become familiar with the most frequent traps Scrum Masters encounter. This chapter will cover how they appear in real life and practical approaches to get past them.

Burnout

Burnout is a slow leak, so it's never a single event. For teams and individuals, it appears as chronic fatigue, cynicism, and decreased performance. For Scrum Masters, burnout usually has two sources:

1. **Relentless Cadence Without Recovery:** Agile's iterative rhythm (sprints, reviews, retrospectives) is energizing when balanced with space to reflect and recover. Without intentional breaks and psychological safety, teams feel compelled to produce sprint after sprint without pause for learning or maintenance. Such pressure can drain energy and motivation in a few months.[54]

---

[54] Saji, Linsa. "Overcoming Agile Challenges with Pragmatic Agile." Nimblework, 9 Aug. 2024, www.nimblework.com/blog/agile-challenges-with-pragmatic-agile. Accessed 9 Jan. 2026.

2. **Carrying the Weight of the Transformation Alone:** Scrum Masters are the voice for change. Leaders look to them for answers, teams rely on them for facilitation, and stakeholders pressure them for progress. When the role expectations outstrip the authority and support given, Scrum Masters end up absorbing stress without support, which leads to a sure path to burnout.

How to Spot It Early

- Constantly reactive work. You feel like you're putting out fires all day.
- Drop in curiosity or experimentation.
- Team morale dips, and sarcastic humor replaces constructive banter.
- You think about leaving the role more often than staying.

How to Address Burnout

Burnout doesn't go away if you push harder. Here are some practical approaches that can help:

Think it Over

Use a retrospective to surface team fatigue as a real impediment. Don't treat stress as a "soft topic," as it affects delivery and innovation.

Delegate and Empower

Empower other team members to share facilitation duties (e.g., have the team rotate who leads retrospectives).

Escalate When Needed

If burnout is systemic (not just one team), escalate it to leadership with tangible data (e.g., declining output, rising defects, absenteeism). Doing this protects you *and* the team.

Burnout is a signal that the way of working needs repair. Lean into those signals with curiosity instead of guilt.

Cargo Cult Agile

One of the most common pitfalls Scrum Masters see is what the industry calls cargo cult Agile. It usually occurs when teams or organizations do the ceremonies, such as daily stand-ups, sprint planning, retros, and yet none of the deeper benefits ever seem to materialize. The Agile rituals are performed, but the mindset behind them is absent.

Cargo cult Agile is mostly a result of misunderstanding. Leaders adopt the visible parts of Agile without changing the invisible ones, i.e., culture, decision rights, autonomy, and feedback loops.[55]

Signs You're in Cargo Cult Mode

- Stand-ups feel like status updates for a manager.
- Metrics like velocity are tracked religiously, but customer value feels invisible.
- Sprint planning is a guessing game rather than a strategy session.
- Retrospectives happen, but the same problems appear in every sprint.

Why This Happens

Surface-level adoption comes from:

- Leadership wanting predictability without changing how decisions are made.
- Teams learning only the mechanics of Agile, not the purpose of iteration and learning.

---

[55] "The Agile Paradox." Scrum.org, 2025, www.scrum.org/resources/blog/agile-paradox.

- Fear of autonomy leading people to cling to ceremonies as a substitute for empowerment.

How to Counter It

Reconnect to Values
Bring the Agile Manifesto principles back into conversations. Regularly ask, *"How is this activity helping us deliver customer value or learn faster?"*

Move from Output to Outcome
A ceremony should produce insight or value. Track customer satisfaction, cycle time, or business impact.

Educate Leaders
Run guided sessions for managers on the difference between performing a stand-up and using stand-ups to coordinate and reveal blockers early.

Turn Ceremonies into Conversations
Retrospectives should lead to experiments with clear owners and deadlines instead of becoming venting sessions.

When Scrum is more than rituals, teams produce value; otherwise, all you have is motion without meaning.

Resistance to Change

Agile invites changes in how people think about work, decisions, and accountability. That can feel threatening to people used to command-and-control structures. Resistance can come from:

- Middle managers uncomfortable with empowerment and ambiguity.
- Developers who felt safe with detailed specifications and now face uncertainty.

- Stakeholders fearful of losing control over timelines and budgets.

Typical Forms of Resistance

- Teams reverting to waterfall habits when deadlines press.
- Managers demanding detailed status reports or rigid plans.
- Scrum Masters being asked to enforce plans rather than facilitate learning.

How to Respond

When to Push

Push when the team or stakeholders are clearly causing harm to flow or value creation. For example:

- Ignoring feedback loops that repeatedly cause defects.
- Replacing retrospectives with status meetings.

In these cases, you need to clearly articulate the risk and propose a different way that ties directly to outcomes.

When to Coach

- Coach when resistance comes from:
- Lack of understanding of Agile intent.
- Fear of making decisions without detailed specs.

In these cases, your work is listening, asking questions, and guiding people to discover better ways for themselves.

Here are some great examples of coaching questions:

- "What outcomes are we expecting this sprint?"
- "What hypothesis are we testing here?"
- "How will we know if this approach worked?"

Coaching helps people internalize change instead of complying with it blindly.

When to Escalate

Escalate when:

- Organizational impediments are beyond your authority to remove.
- Leadership continues to block essential Agile practices.

Escalation isn't the same as tattling. In fact, it is a form of highlighting critical risks before they cause systemic failure. Bring data, examples, and possible options — not just problems.

One common organizational resistance is the belief that Agile means less planning or documentation. When people misunderstand flexibility, it leads to scope creep and a lack of accountability. As a result, there exist many hindrances to progress. In such cases, it is essential to connect Agile practices to business outcomes so that conversations can change directions.

Micromanagement and Role Confusion

Micromanagement Pitfalls

Scrum Masters sometimes fall into the trap of micromanaging the team or acting as a pseudo-project manager. This kills autonomy, undermines learning, and stifles creativity.[56]

Clarity of Role

Scrum Masters facilitate flow, remove impediments, and coach autonomy. They do not assign tasks, enforce individual

---

[56] GitScrum Tribes. "Scrum Master Anti-Patterns: Avoid Agile Pitfalls." GitScrum Tribes, 27 Apr. 2025, tribes.gitscrum.com/scrum-master-pitfalls-steer-clear-of-anti-patterns-optimize-agile-flow. Accessed 12 Jan. 2026.

productivity measures, or track attendance. Clarity around this distinction prevents resentment and role conflict.

These pitfalls aren't unique or rare. They're common because agility challenges powerful habits that have been with organizations for decades. The work of the Scrum Master is to illuminate these patterns, encourage learning, and co-create structures that support flow, autonomy, and value creation.

Every pitfall contains some form of information. When teams get stuck, that's where the richest data lives. Skilled Scrum Masters mine that data, help teams learn from it, and use those lessons to change how work is carried out.

Chapter 11 – The Business Impact Playbook

You have learned about Scrum Masters as strategic leaders, metrics that matter, career paths and common pitfalls. Now you need practical materials you can use right away, i.e., templates, checklists, facilitation guides, ways to measure your impact clearly, and guidance on how to communicate your contributions to stakeholders and leaders.

So, by the end of this chapter, you will have a clear understanding of how to become a business-critical Scrum Master whose work turns into visible value for the team and the organization.

Templates, Checklists, and Facilitation Guides

Templates and checklists help you bring structure to work that is otherwise invisible. They reduce guesswork, accelerate onboarding for new teams, make conversations less awkward, and ensure that important topics are not skipped. Facilitation guides, on the other hand, make your meetings purposeful instead of routine.

Below you will find core artifacts every Scrum Master should use or adapt:

Team Value Canvas

A simple one-page canvas helps teams align work with customer and business outcomes. Before every considerable effort or quarterly plan, run a value canvas session.[57]

Sections of the Value Canvas

Customer Outcomes: What real change are we trying to produce for the customer?

- **Business Outcomes:** How will the business benefit if those customer outcomes happen?
- **Measures of Success:** What evidence will tell us we are making progress?
- **Risks and Assumptions:** What might stop us from achieving outcomes?
- **Sprint Goals:** What will we deliver this sprint that moves us forward?

This format ensures the team is not just building a list of features but thinking about why those features matter now.

Evidence-Based Metrics Board

Use a joint board (physical or digital) where you collect and visualize metrics that reflect business value and learning.

Include:

- **Current Value Indicators**. For example, customer satisfaction trends.
- **Ability to Innovate Indicators** such as experiment success rates.

---

[57] Ivanov, Alexey. "Team Canvas Complete: Instructions - Alexey Ivanov - Medium." Medium, Medium, 7 July 2023, helloalexivanov.medium.com/team-canvas-complete-instructions-e6f33bc9b29f.

- **Time to Market Indicators**. It measures related to cycle time and lead time.
- **Unrealized Value Indicators.** These are opportunities identified but not yet delivered.

This structure is the core of the Evidence-Based Management (EBM) framework and helps teams track value rather than just activity. Organize sessions every sprint to update the board and reflect on trends. [58]

Sprint Goal Alignment Checklist

Here's a quick checklist to use during Sprint Planning to keep your Scrum Team aligned with customer and business outcomes:

- Did the team agree on one clear goal for this sprint?
- Does this goal link to a real customer outcome?
- Is there a measure we can expect to see shift if the goal is achieved?
- Are dependencies and risks surfaced and addressed?
- Is the Product Owner confident that this goal supports business priorities?

Using this checklist strengthens the team's ability to focus on outcomes. It also makes Sprint Reviews more meaningful because progress is assessed against a collective purpose.

Retrospective Outcome Action Plan Template

Retrospectives are where improvement happens. Use this template to capture insights and make them actionable.

Retrospective Action Plan
- **Observation**: What happened?

---

[58] "How to Measure Value with Evidence-Based Management." Scrum.org, 2021, www.scrum.org/resources/how-measure-value-evidence-based-management.

- **Impact**: What effect did it have on our work or results?
- **Root Cause**: Why did this occur?
- **Experiment**: What action will we take next sprint?
- **Success Measure**: How will we know this experiment worked?
- **Owner**: Who is responsible?

The Success Measure line forces you to define evidence before the improvement cycle even begins. Over time, you will build a portfolio of experiments and outcomes that show growth.

Stakeholder Communication Plan

This tool helps you prepare and structure conversations with key business partners. It includes:

- **Audience**: Who are you talking to?
- **Goal of the Conversation**: What do you need from them?
- **Evidence or Story:** What data or example supports your request?
- **Expected Outcome**: What decision or action do you want?
- **Follow-Up Plan**: How will you follow through?

This is one of the simplest tools that makes your value visible to others because it turns intuition into a business conversation with clear evidence and purpose.

Risk and Opportunity Radar

Use the risk and opportunity radar to capture risks and opportunities weekly. Classify items by likelihood or impact and assign a next-step action.

This board becomes a central artifact for Sprint Reviews, Release Planning, and conversations with leadership about impediments and opportunities.

How to Measure and Communicate Your Impact

Measuring and communicating impact is one of the most complex skills for Scrum Masters. Internal teams may see your influence clearly, but leadership and executives respond to simple narratives backed by evidence.

Your job is to build connections between what you do with teams and what the business cares about. Let's take a more detailed look:

Define What Counts as Impact in Your Context

Before you measure impact, clarify what success means for your team and organization. Every context is different, so work with your Product Owner and leaders to define what matters.

Impact typically appears in three areas:

1. Delivery Performance

Metrics here show how predictable and reliable delivery is. Examples include cycle time, lead time, throughput, defect escape rates, and sprint goal reliability. These tell the business that the team can be trusted to deliver value consistently.

2. Business Results

High-level business outcomes like customer satisfaction, revenue impact, retention, decreased cost of delay, or reduced support tickets are metrics leaders value. These require collaboration with product management and business owners.

3. Team and Organizational Health

Engaged, stable, and high-learning teams are more likely to produce value over time. Use regular pulse checks or happiness surveys and watch trends over months. These measures provide evidence of sustainable performance.

Use Evidence-Based Management (EBM)

As mentioned earlier, EBM is a framework that helps teams measure value rather than effort. The framework calls for tracking four areas:

1. **Current Value**: How much value the product delivers now.
2. **Unrealized Value**: The potential value not yet delivered.
3. **Ability to Innovate**: How capable the organization is at creating new value.
4. **Time to Market**: How quickly the organization learns from feedback.

Use these categories in your dashboards, team boards, and Sprint Reviews so that the conversation surrounds outcomes instead of output.

For example, track how long it takes to deliver customer requests and how often releases result in positive customer feedback. Over time, leaders will see a pattern in the data that connects work with measurable business results.

Frame Data With a Narrative

Numbers alone do not move decisions. You must provide context and explanation.

A simple story structure works well:

- **Condition**: This is where we started.
- **Action**: This is what we did.
- **Outcome:** This is what changed.
- **Evidence**: This is how we know.

In Sprint Reviews and stakeholder meetings, present data using this structure. It helps others understand whether change comes from your actions or from other factors.

For example:

- ***Condition***: *Sprint goal reliability was 40% the last three quarters.*
- ***Action***: *We adjusted sprint planning, clarified producer and stakeholder expectations, and used outcome indicator boards.*
- ***Outcome***: *Reliability increased to 75% over six sprints.*
- ***Evidence***: *Board visuals, cadence reports, and retrospective outcomes.*

This format clarifies your contribution without unnecessary technical jargon.

Build a Report Card for Your Team

Create a simple quarterly report card you can share with leadership. Include:

- A summary of measures under EBM categories.
- Trends over time.
- Improvements made and experiments run.
- Decisions enabled and risks mitigated.

This report card becomes a tool for conversations with executives and boosts visibility of your impact beyond the team.

Be Intentional With Language

When presenting metrics, avoid building false precision. If a number is rough or an estimate, say so. Leaders will respect honesty more than polished but meaningless numbers.

Always tie your metrics back to behaviors and decisions. Metrics are meaningful only if they lead to better decisions and learning.

How to Facilitate Evidence Conversations With Stakeholders

Many Scrum Masters struggle to communicate with stakeholders in a language that resonates. These conversations go best when you shift from reporting metrics to facilitating decision moments.

Set Up Quarterly Value Review Workshops

Workshops bring together team representatives, product owners, and business stakeholders to inspect progress and set direction for the next quarter.

Agenda:

- Present your EBM dashboard.
- Review trends in each category.
- Discuss the three biggest risks and opportunities.
- Agree on two experiments for the next quarter.

Workshops give leaders a role in influencing future work rather than simply reviewing past activity.

Facilitate Risk-Based Conversations

Create a regular short forum where risks and opportunities are discussed in a structured manner.

Use a simple agenda:

- List known risks.
- Prioritize by impact and likelihood.
- Decide on mitigation actions.
- Assign owners.

This keeps attention on what matters and makes impediments visible early.

Run Decision Workshops Before Each Major Increment

Before major releases, run workshops where teams and leaders align on:

- What problem is solved?
- What hypotheses are being tested?
- What evidence is needed to consider this increment a success?

This impacts expectations and prevents misalignment between teams and executives.

A Final Call to Action: Become a Business-Critical Scrum Master

Throughout this book, one message has been consistent. The Scrum Master role has grown far beyond facilitating events or protecting calendars. Today, Scrum Masters impact workflows, decisions, and how organizations learn. When done well, the role directly influences outcomes that leaders and customers care about.

Of course, becoming a business-critical Scrum Master does not happen by accident or overnight. It happens when you choose to work with intention. It happens when you stop measuring success only by how well Scrum runs and start measuring it by how clearly the organization can see, decide, and adapt.

That change demands a few core habits. You need the discipline to focus on outcomes, not activity. You need evidence to ground conversations in reality instead of opinion. You need the courage to speak up when learning is replaced by guesswork or when teams are being pushed to deliver without clarity.

So, start your journey today.

Start this week by defining the impact measures that matter most to your team and stakeholders. Make them visible. Talk about them often. Let them guide conversations instead of letting assumptions drive decisions.

Choose one template or board from the previous chapter and put it to work in your next sprint. Do not aim for perfection. Aim for usefulness. Let the team learn by using it and improving it together.

Before your next leadership or stakeholder meeting, hold one structured value conversation. Bring evidence. Tell a clear story about what is happening, what has changed, and what decisions are needed next. These conversations build trust over time and change how people experience your role.

Lead at least one experiment with a clear hypothesis and outcome measure. Treat learning as real work, not a side activity. Even small experiments send a powerful message that improvement is expected and supported.

None of this requires special authority or a new title. All you need is curiosity about how the system really works. It requires partnership with your team and respect for the pressures your business partners face. It requires consistency, even when results are not immediate.

As you make the impact more visible, the gap between what teams deliver and what the organization values starts to shrink. Decisions become clearer. Conversations turn calmer. Teams gain confidence, and leaders gain trust in the system.

Over time, people will seek you out. Not because you run good meetings, but because you help them see reality, navigate uncertainty, and move forward with confidence.

That is the point where your work becomes indispensable.

When you master these habits, you are no longer simply supporting Agile ways of working. You are helping teams thrive and enabling organizations to make better choices in complex environments.

That is exactly what it means to be a business-critical Scrum Master.

www.ingramcontent.com/pod-product-compliance
Lightning Source LLC
Chambersburg PA
CBHW050505210326
41521CB00011B/2337